Knitting
Stitches

VISUAL™
ENCYCLOPEDIA

350 Stitch Patterns, Edgings, and More

Sharon Turner

WILEY

John Wiley & Sons, Inc.

Credits

Acquisitions Editor
Pam Mourouzis

Senior Project Editor
Donna Wright

Copy Editor
Marylouise Wiack

Technical Editor
Kristi Porter

Editorial Manager
Christina Stambaugh

Vice President and Publisher
Cindy Kitchel

Vice President and Executive Publisher
Kathy Nebenhaus

Interior Design
Jennifer Mayberry

Photography
Matt Bowen

Special Thanks...

To the following knitters for all of their beautiful handwork—if it weren't for all of your help at the last minute, I would have been knitting swatches until the end of time.

- Anne Berk
- Gina Kanouse
- Simone Payment
- Annie Rota

About the Author

Sharon Turner is the author of *Teach Yourself Visually Knitting, Teach Yourself Visually Knitting Design, Knitting Visual Quick Tips, Find Your Style and Knit It Too,* and *Monkeysuits: Sweaters and More to Knit for Kids.* When her daughters were babies, Sharon published Monkeysuits, a line of knitting patterns for babies and children. She lives in Brooklyn, New York, and Hague, New York with her husband and three daughters. In Summer 2011, Sharon graduated from nursing school and became a registered nurse.

Acknowledgments

When Pam Mourouzis—the very talented Acquisitions Editor at Wiley Publishing—and I first spoke about this *Knitting Visual Stitches Encyclopedia*, we agreed it would probably be "pretty easy." Once underway, it emerged as something more complex than originally envisioned. (And it didn't help that I was finishing up my last year of nursing school, and preparing for my licensure exam.) Throughout the entire process, Pam, and Donna Wright, Senior Project Editor Extraordinaire, worked diligently to see this intricate project through to fruition. And even though I got more and more behind, Donna and Pam never seemed to lose patience; instead, they always offered support and more time. Thank you, Pam, for the privilege of working on this book. And Donna, you deserve the highest commendation for deftly sorting the bits and pieces that trickled in (at too slow a pace), and for building a comprehensive—and comprehensible—finished book out of it all.

I am forever grateful to Kristi Porter, Technical Editor (and author of several knitting books herself), for sharing and applying her vast knitting and pattern-writing knowledge to ensure that this book's patterns make sense. Kristi's remarkable ability to pay close attention to millions of tiny details while simultaneously maintaining a clear view of the big picture has been invaluable. Thank you, Kristi.

Many knitters worked their fingers to the bone to fill these pages with colorful swatches. My dear friend, Brenda Adelson, devoted many of her evening hours to help create many of the knit swatches shown in the book. Another dear friend and Brooklyn neighbor, Yuki Sahara, knitted a zillion swatches and was always sure to point out errors or odd wording that could be confusing. Pam Mourouzis, who already has a full plate, also expertly knit many of the swatches shown and made sure to let everyone know how much she enjoyed it. My sister Lauren (Doll) and my pal Kristen also knit some swatches when they weren't distracted by their own busy lives, and I'm so thankful to them for that. Isabel, my eldest daughter, also took time from her demanding school schedule to help out and knit a few swatches. Applause goes to Matt Bowen for photographing and re-photographing so many little knit squares so that they looked just right. Thanks also to Mary Louise Wiack for her eagle-eyed review early on; to Christina Stambaugh for expertly directing the production of this exhaustive project so that all of the details came together in one neat package; and to Wiley Publisher Cindy Kitchel for allowing me the opportunity to work on this intricate project.

To my best advisor and husband Mark, and to our three delightful daughters Isabel, Matilda, and Phoebe—you are the best.

Table of Contents

CHAPTER 1 Knit and Purl Patterns 1

Seed Stitch

CHAPTER 2 Rib Patterns 37

2 x 2 Rib

CHAPTER 3 Bobbles and Textured Stitches 61

Star Stitch

Table of Contents

CHAPTER 4 Slipstitch Patterns 77

Heel Stitch

CHAPTER 5 Twist-Stitch Patterns 91

Medium Braid

CHAPTER 6   Cable Patterns   108

Big Cable

Table of Contents

CHAPTER 7   Drop-stitch, Yarn Overs, Eyelet, and Lace   142

Eyelet Chevrons

Basic Ruffle

Feather and Fan Cable Panel

Strand Color 7

Table of Contents

Introduction

This encyclopedia offers 350 knitting stitches: simple knits and purls; intricate ribbed, bobbled, slipped, twisted, and cabled stitches; lace, edgings, and colorwork. Use the book to explore new patterns, to practice unfamiliar techniques, or to design and create distinctive hand-knit sweaters, accessories, and items to decorate your home.

Before You Begin

You'll need to know that all of the stitch patterns come complete with a detailed color photo and clear, simple, stitch-by-stitch instructions. In addition, all but a few of the patterns are represented in chart form. (Refer to the Appendix to clarify stitch maneuvers and interpret the symbols and charts.) When applying the patterns to your own designs, knit a sample swatch (or two or three or four) to see if the stitch pattern has the right texture, weight, and drape for your project. The type of yarn you use—the fiber and how it is spun—impacts the outcome tremendously. Many pure wool yarns are elastic and have a lot of body. Cotton, linen, bamboo, and other plant-based yarns do not have a lot of stretch. Fuzzy, hairy, slubby, and loosely spun yarns can either conceal or accentuate a stitch pattern, so you'll definitely have to experiment with those. Tightly spun yarns worked on the right size needles generally offer effective stitch definition if that's what you're after. The sample swatches shown in the photographs were knit in a lightweight yarn for consistency and stitch clarity. Explore the whole range of yarn weights when making your samples. Knit a bobbled cable in a super-bulky wool, work lace in medium cotton on big needles, or try an intricate knit and purl pattern on tiny needles in superfine silk, and watch the stitch pattern swell or contract. When designing projects that are gauge-sensitive, knit a fairly large gauge swatch to ensure accuracy. Remember that different stitch patterns produce a wide variety of fabrics, ranging from dense and stiff to soft and loose.

How This Book Is Organized

Here is a brief summary of the types of patterns that you can knit using this book.

Chapter 1: Knit and Purl Patterns

This chapter is the most straightforward in terms of technique and level of skill required. But don't skip it if you're a knitter who likes a challenge, because this chapter includes over 50 stitch patterns, many of them intricate and inspiring.

Chapter 2: Rib Patterns

You'll find a variety of rib patterns in this chapter: some comprised of simple knits and purls, and others that take you beyond the basics to eye-catching ribs that use eyelets, slipped and twisted stitches, and textural shaping maneuvers. Many of the patterns here are not just for cuffs, borders, and hems. So if an elastic ribbed sock or hat is what you're making, be sure to test the stitch pattern to make sure it's that type of rib.

Chapter 3: Bobbles and Textured Stitches

This chapter offers an array of bumpy, knotty, woven, and wavy stitches. Many of these patterns require more yarn per square inch than the simpler knit and purl patterns. When planning your project, consider knitting a 4-inch square swatch in your chosen yarn and stitch pattern, then unravel the swatch and measure how many yards of yarn you used. Calculate yards per square inch by dividing the number of yards of yarn your 4-inch square swatch used by 16. Take that number and multiply it by what you estimate to be your project's area in square inches, and you should have a pretty good idea of how many yards of that particular yarn you'll need. (Actually, you can estimate yardage this way for stitch patterns in any of the chapters.)

Chapter 4: Slipstitch Patterns

Slipstitch knitting is one of the most satisfying knitting techniques; Most of the patterns are quicker to work, yet result in fascinating, dynamic, and eye-pleasing designs. And many slipstitch patterns more closely resemble weaving than knitting. Regarding the mechanics of slipping stitches, stitches are always slipped purlwise unless otherwise noted. You'll often see the abbreviations *wyif* and *wyib*—referring to where the yarn is held when slipping a stitch—*wyif* means the yarn is held in front of the stitch being slipped, and *wyib* means the yarn is held in back of the stitch being slipped. In this book, *wyif* and *wyib* make no reference to the right side or the wrong side of the work; rather, they refer to the placement of the yarn relative to the stitch on the left needle, regardless of whether you're working a right side or wrong side row. Because slipping stitches tends to pull the knitting tightly together, the resulting fabric of some of the slipstitch patterns can be rather dense and inelastic. Certain patterns require larger needles to manage this increased tension. Hold the yarn in a relaxed and comfortable fashion, so that the natural tightening tendency doesn't make knitting difficult, and enjoy experimenting with a variety of yarns and needle sizes.

Chapter 5: Twist-Stitch Patterns

You'll get a taste of how versatile twist-stitch knitting can be using the patterns in this chapter. Knitting or purling into the back loops of the stitches, or knitting or purling the second stitch on the needle before the first stitch, allows you to generate designs with wandering stitches and linear graphics that rival cables (without having to wrestle with a cable needle). On the other hand, you can also work simple 2-stitch, 2-row twist-stitch patterns that form captivating textures. As with many stitch patterns, you'll want to knit a good size sample swatch to accurately measure gauge, as twist-stitches tighten your knitting, resulting in a measurement that requires more stitches per inch.

Chapter 6: Cable Patterns

Many knitters prefer knitting cables above all other types of knitting. Cables can be sleek and simple, like the basic right and left cable—worked over just four or six rows—or exquisitely complex, forming ornate, even sculptural relief over many stitches and rows. Use these patterns to hone your cabling skills, or pair them with textural stitch patterns from earlier chapters to design your own cable-knit sweaters and accessories. Accurately measuring gauge with cables can be tricky, especially if you're combining many cables into one elaborately knit item. As always, take time to knit samples. And if you're the type of knitter who doesn't want a project that requires intense concentration and continuous counting of stitches and rows, try working a single cable as an accent to a sleek design.

Chapter 7: Drop-stitch, Yarn Overs, Eyelet, and Lace

This chapter offers a variety of stitch patterns that share the trait of intentionally creating holes in the fabric to form the design, and the patterns are wonderful when worked in the lighter weight yarns. Fine cottons, linens, and silks lend themselves beautifully to openwork. Scarves, shawls, and throws are perfect vehicles for intricate lace patterns because they don't require keeping track of intricate shaping and complex stitch patterns at the same time. After knitting your sample swatches, be sure to stretch them (and even pin, if necessary) to open up the holes before blocking. This will ensure that the pattern is visible at its best. Explore these lacy, airy patterns by knitting 8-inch by 8-inch openwork samples in dishcloth cotton—you'll master more open stitches in less time, plus you'll have some lovely washcloths to keep or give as gifts.

Chapter 8: Borders and Edgings

This chapter provides you with a sampling of designs to ornament your knitting. Some of these can be worked from the bottom up, so that when the border or edging is complete, you can just keep knitting your item from there. Others are knit lengthwise, and so must be worked separately to the same length as the edge to which they will be attached. The majority of the swatches for this chapter were knit in lightweight cotton to accentuate the lacy patterns, but you should experiment with other fibers and weights.

Chapter 9: Creative Stitches and Combinations

As the title suggests, this chapter includes patterns that employ multiple techniques—more than one cable in a panel, bobbles and eyelets in the same design, or patterns that employ unusual stitches and maneuvers. Use this chapter as a stepping-stone to designing your own creative combinations.

Chapter 10: Color Knitting

There are many forms of color knitting. You will find patterns for stranded knitting—frequently referred to as Fair Isle knitting—as well as several intarsia motifs and color-slip designs. These patterns are presented in easy-to-follow color charts; you can follow the colors presented, or simply use the charts as inspiration and select your own color combinations.

Stranded knitting involves using two colors in one row, carrying both colors across the back of the work. Take care that the yarns stranded on the wrong side are not too taut, or your work will pucker. Some of these stitches form allover patterns made up entirely of two colors. Other allover designs use three, four, five, or more different colors. There are also stranded designs for borders, floral patterns, nautical motifs, and modern geometric configurations. Mix and match these to create your own unique colorwork.

Intarsia knitting involves scattering isolated blocks of color or motifs over the knit field. You work each motif with a separate ball or bobbin of yarn. When it's time to change colors—from background color to motif color, for example—twist the yarns together on the wrong side to avoid ending up with holes on the right side. For motifs that have only a few stitches in a particular color—a bird's beak, a dog's nose, for example—you can cheat and work those bits in duplicate stitch. Knit these intarsia "stitch pictures" into sweaters, hats, pillow cushions, and more to individualize your knit projects.

Color-slip knitting patterns close the chapter, and if you've never worked color-slip knitting, you should definitely give it a try. After stripes, it's the easiest form of color knitting. This technique is a wonderful way to work with two colors at the same time, without stranding or using bobbins. You work one color at a time in each row, using the same color over the first two consecutive rows, while slipping the stitches that would normally be worked in the second color. For the following two rows, you work with the second color, and slip the stitches that would be worked in the first color. Also, you can work color-slip knitting in garter stitch for a bumpy texture and compressed version of the pattern, and stockinette stitch for a smoother fabric and elongated version of the color design.

Note on the Color-Slip Charts: Each row of a color-slip chart is labeled with an odd number on the right, and an even number on the left. That's because each chart row stands for the two rows worked in one color. The odd numbers represent the right side rows and are read from right to left, and the even numbers represent the wrong side rows and are read from left to right. On the right and left edges of the chart you will see a column of black and white checks. These are not part of the actual stitch pattern; rather, they are a key to which color is worked for the two rows that the one chart row represents. If the row has a black square at its beginning, then the darker color is the working color, and the lighter color is the slipped color. The same will be true for the corresponding wrong side row. All of the charts here begin with the darker color. In order to have the light-colored stitches to slip in that first row, cast on in the lighter color and work two plain rows. Attach your darker color, and you're ready to begin working the pattern from the chart.

And Now, the Fun Part . . .

Gather several balls of yarn in your favorite colors and fibers, collect a few different-sized needles and essential knitting notions, and put them and this book into your favorite knitting bag. Don't forget to take along a pencil and graph paper for inventing and charting your own stitch patterns. Go find a comfortable spot that's quiet enough to hear the soothing clicking of your needles, and light enough to watch exquisite fabrics emerge as you knit.

CHAPTER 1

Knit and Purl Patterns

Garter Stitch

Garter stitch is the easiest stitch pattern, and what's great about it is that it always lies perfectly flat. It looks exactly the same on both the front and the back.

Cast on any number of sts.

Row 1: Knit.

Rep row 1 for garter stitch.

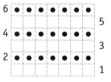

Stockinette Stitch

Stockinette stitch is the pattern most often used for sweaters. The right side looks like rows of flat Vs; the wrong side looks like rows of bumps.

Cast on any number of sts.

Row 1 (RS): Knit.

Row 2 (WS): Purl.

Rep rows 1 and 2 for stockinette stitch.

Reverse Stockinette Stitch

Reverse stockinette stitch is the same as regular stockinette, only the bumpy side is considered the right side, and the smooth side is the wrong side.

Cast on any number of sts.

Row 1 (RS): Purl.

Row 2 (WS): Knit.

Rep rows 1 and 2 for reverse stockinette stitch.

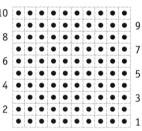

Garter Stitch Stripe

This pattern is made up of two rows of stockinette stitch and two rows of garter stitch. You can vary the number of rows of stockinette stitch and garter stitch to create your own stripe pattern.

Cast on any number of sts.

Row 1 (RS): Knit.

Row 2 (WS): Purl.

Rows 3 and 4: Knit.

Rep rows 1–4 for garter stitch stripe.

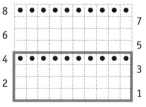

Reverse Stockinette Stitch Stripe

This pattern looks similar to garter stitch stripe, but because the bumpy stripes are done in reverse stockinette stitch, they are fuller and rounder.

Cast on any number of sts.

Row 1 (RS): Knit.

Row 2 (WS): Purl.

Row 3: Knit.

Rows 4 and 5: Purl.

Row 6: Knit.

Rep rows 1–6 for reverse stockinette stitch stripe.

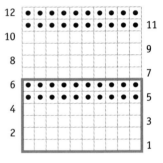

Seed Stitch

Seed stitch creates a nice bumpy-textured fabric that lies flat and looks the same on both sides. You knit the purl stitches and purl the knit stitches.

Cast on an even number of sts.

Row 1 (RS): *K1, p1; rep from * to end.

Row 2 (WS): *P1, k1; rep from * to end.

Rep rows 1 and 2 for seed stitch.

Double Seed Stitch

Double seed stitch, sometimes called moss stitch, is a four-row version of seed stitch.

Cast on an even number of sts.

Row 1 (RS): *K1, p1; rep from * to end.

Row 2 (WS): Rep row 1.

Rows 3 and 4: *P1, k1; rep from * to end.

Rep rows 1–4 for double seed stitch.

Simple Seed Stitch

Simple seed stitch is a good allover pattern for sweaters, vests, and dresses.

Cast on a multiple of 4 sts plus 1.

Row 1 (RS): P1, *k3, p1; rep from * to end.

Row 2 and all even-numbered rows (WS): Purl.

Row 3: Knit.

Row 5: K2, p1, *k3, p1; rep from * to last 2 sts, k2.

Row 7: Knit.

Row 8: Purl.

Rep rows 1–8 for simple seed stitch.

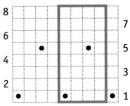

Box Stitch

Box stitch looks the same on both sides and lies flat.

Cast on a multiple of 4 sts plus 2.

Row 1 (RS): K2, *p2, k2; rep from * to end.

Row 2 (WS): P2, *k2, p2; rep from * to end.

Row 3: Rep row 2.

Row 4: Rep row 1.

Rep rows 1–4 for box stitch.

Andalusian Stitch

This stitch, which creates a nice grid pattern, is easy to do.

Cast on a multiple of 2 sts plus 1.

Row 1 (RS): Knit.

Row 2 (WS): Purl.

Row 3: *K1, p1; rep from * to last st, k1.

Row 4: Purl.

Rep rows 1–4 for Andalusian stitch.

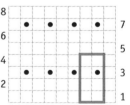

Checkerboard

This pattern looks the same on both sides, so it's great for blankets, scarves, and wraps.

Cast on a multiple of 8 sts plus 4.

Rows 1 and 3 (RS): K4, *p4, k4; rep from * to end.

Rows 2 and 4 (WS): P4, *k4, p4; rep from * to end.

Rows 5 and 7: Rep row 2.

Rows 6 and 8: Rep row 1.

Rep rows 1–8 for checkerboard pattern.

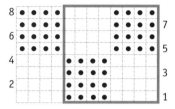

Rice Stitch

This easy allover pattern lies flat and looks like ribbing on the wrong side.

Cast on a multiple of 2 sts plus 1.

Row 1 (RS): P1, *k1 tbl, p1; rep from * to end.

Row 2 (WS): Knit.

Rep rows 1 and 2 for rice stitch.

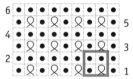

Triangle Check

Here's an easy pattern that's reversible and looks great as a border or an allover pattern.

Cast on a multiple of 6 sts plus 5.

Row 1: K5, *p1, k5; rep from * to end.

Rows 2 and 5: K1, *p3, k3; rep from *, end p3, k1.

Rows 3 and 4: P2, *k1, p5; rep from *, end k1, p2.

Row 6: Rep row 1.

Rep rows 1–6 for triangle check.

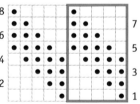

Diagonal Check

Here is another reversible check pattern that works beautifully for blankets, throws, and scarves.

Cast on a multiple of 5 sts.

Row 1 (RS): *P1, k4; rep from * to end.

Row 2 (WS): *P3, k2; rep from * to end.

Row 3: Rep row 2.

Row 4: Rep row 1.

Row 5: *K1, p4; rep from * to end.

Row 6: *K3, p2; rep from * to end.

Row 7: Rep row 6.

Row 8: Rep row 5.

Rep rows 1–8 for diagonal check.

Diamond Brocade

This is an elegant allover pattern.

Cast on a multiple of 8 sts plus 1.

Row 1 (RS): K4, *p1, k7; rep from * to last 5 sts, p1, k4.

Rows 2 and 8 (WS): P3, *k1, p1, k1, p5; rep from * to last 6 sts, k1, p1, k1, p3.

Rows 3 and 7: K2, *p1, k3; rep from * to last 3 sts, p1, k2.

Rows 4 and 6: P1, *k1, p5, k1, p1; rep from * to end.

Row 5: *P1, k7; rep from * to last st, p1.

Row 8: P3, *k1, p1, k1, p5; rep from * to last 6 sts, k1, p1, k1, p3.

Rep rows 1–8 for diamond brocade.

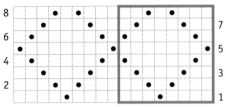

Diamonds in Columns

You can repeat any motif in a series of panels. This one works well on sweaters, vests, and pillows.

Cast on a multiple of 8 sts plus 1.

Row 1 (RS): Knit.

Row 2 (WS): K1, *p7, k1; rep from * to end.

Rows 3 and 7: K4, *p1, k7; rep from * to last 5 sts, p1, k4.

Rows 4 and 6: K1, *p2, k1, p1, k1, p2, k1; rep from * to end.

Row 5: K2, *[p1, k1] twice, p1, k3; rep from * to last 7 sts, [p1, k1] twice, p1, k2.

Row 8: K1, *p7, k1; rep from * to end.

Rep rows 1–8 for diamonds in columns.

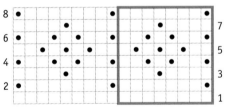

Single Chevron Stitch

Single chevron stitch is a playful pattern that works well on pullovers, cardigans, and vests.

Cast on a multiple of 8 sts.

Row 1 (RS): *P1, k3; rep from * to end.

Row 2 (WS): *K1, p5, k1, p1; rep from * to end.

Row 3: *K2, p1, k3, p1, k1; rep from * to end.

Row 4: *P2, k1, p1, k1, p3; rep from * to end.

Rep rows 1–4 for single chevron stitch.

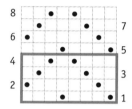

Vertical Dash Stitch

Vertical dash stitch works well as an allover pattern for sweaters, skirts, and dresses.

Cast on a multiple of 6 sts plus 1.

Rows 1 and 3 (RS): P3, k1, *p5, k1; rep from * to last 3 sts, p3.

Rows 2 and 4 (WS): K3, p1, *k5, p1; rep from * to last 3 sts, k3.

Rows 5 and 7: K1, *p5, k1; rep from * to end.

Rows 6 and 8: P1, *k5, p1; rep from * to end.

Rep rows 1–8 for vertical dash stitch.

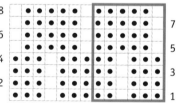

Dotted Lines

The knotted accent dresses up this simple p3, k1 pattern.

Cast on a multiple of 4 sts plus 3.

Rows 1 and 3 (RS): P3, *k1, p3; rep from * to end.

Rows 2 and 4: K3, *p1, k3; rep from * to end.

Row 5: P3, *[k1, yo, k1] in next st, p3; rep from * to end.

Row 6: K3, *p3tog, k3; rep from * to end.

Rep rows 1–6 for dotted lines.

Flowered Columns

This pattern is reversible, so there really isn't a right side or a wrong side. The column of flowers looks the same either way, however the backgrounds are different—stockinette stitch on one side, and reverse stockinette on the other.

Cast on a multiple of 8 sts plus 7.

Rows 1 and 9: K3, *p1, k3; rep from * to end.

Row 2: P3, *k1, p3; rep from * to end.

Rows 3 and 7: K2, p1, k1, *[p1, k2] twice, p1, k1; rep from *, end p1, k2.

Rows 4 and 8: P2, k1, p1, *[k1, p2] twice, k1, p1; rep from *, end k1, p2.

Row 5: K1, *p1, k1; rep from * to end.

Row 6: P1, *k1, p1; rep from * to end.

Row 10: P3, *k1, p3; rep from * to end.

Rep rows 1–10 for flowered columns.

Little Windows

A simple arrangement of knit and purl stitches creates these stockinette stitch "windows" on a reverse stockinette stitch background.

Cast on a multiple of 10 sts plus 1.

Rows 1 and 5 (RS): Purl.

Rows 2 and 4: K4, *p3, k7; rep from *, ending last rep with k4.

Row 3: P4, *k3, p7; rep from *, ending last rep with p4.

Row 6: Knit.

Rows 7 and 9: K2, *p7, k3; rep from *, ending last rep with k2.

Row 8: P2, *k7, p3; rep from *, ending last rep with p2.

Row 10: Knit.

Rep rows 1–10 for little windows.

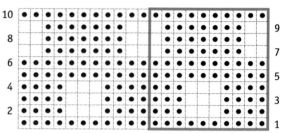

Reversible Diamonds

This big and bold pattern works wonderfully when both sides of the knitted piece are showing. Either side can be the "right side." Play with the scale of the pattern by working reversible diamonds in a bulky or super-bulky yarn.

Cast on a multiple of 12 sts plus 1.

Row 1 (RS): K5, *p3, k9; rep from *, ending last rep k5.

Row 2: P5, *k3, p9; rep from *, ending last rep k5.

Row 3: K4, *p5, k7; rep from *, ending last rep k4.

Row 4: P4, *k5, p7; rep from *, ending last rep k4.

Row 5: K3, *p3, k1, p3, k5; rep from *, ending last rep k3.

Row 6: P3, *k3, p1, k3, p5; rep from *, ending last rep p3.

Row 7: K2, *p3, k3; rep from *, ending last rep k2.

Row 8: P2, *k3, p3; rep from *, ending last rep p2.

Row 9: K1, *p3, k5, p3, k1; rep from * to end.

Row 10: P1, *k3, p5, k3, p1; rep from * to end.

Row 11: P3, *k7, p5; rep from *, ending last rep p3.

Row 12: K3, *p7, k5; rep from *, ending last rep k3.

Row 13: P2, *k9, p3; rep from *, ending last rep p2.

Row 14: K2, *p9, k3; rep from *, ending last rep k2.

Rep rows 1–14 for reversible diamonds.

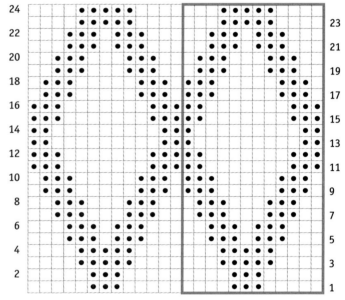

Basketweave I

There are many forms of basketweave. This one creates a small weave.

Cast on a multiple of 5 sts plus 3.

Row 1 (RS): Knit.

Rows 2 and 4 (WS): *K3, p2; rep from * to last 3 sts, k3.

Rows 3, 5, and 7: Knit.

Rows 6 and 8: K1, *p2, k3; rep from * to last 2 sts, p2.

Rep rows 1–8 for basketweave I.

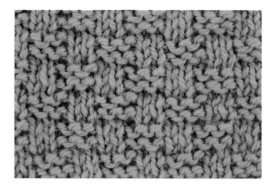

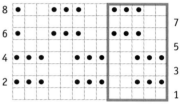

Basketweave II

This basketweave is a bit larger than basketweave I.

Cast on a multiple of 9 sts plus 3.

Rows 1, 3, and 5 (RS): K3, *p6, k3; rep from * to end.

Rows 2, 4, and 6: P3, *k6, p3; rep from * to end.

Rows 7 and 9: P3, *k6, p3; rep from * to end.

Rows 8 and 10: K3, *p6, k3; rep from * to end.

Rep rows 1–10 for basketweave II.

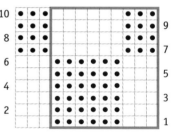

Big Basketweave

The push and pull of the horizontals and verticals in this pattern create a fluid, wavy weave. Let the pattern do what it does naturally, or block for a less curvy look.

Cast on a multiple of 18 sts plus 10.

Rows 1 and 5 (RS): *K11, p2, k2, p2, k1; rep from *, ending with k10.

Rows 2 and 6: P1, k8, p1, *p1, [k2, p2] twice, k8, p1; rep from * to end.

Rows 3 and 7: *K1, p8, [k2, p2] twice, k1; rep from *, ending last rep k1, p8, k1.

Rows 4 and 8: P10, *p1, k2, p2, k2, p11; rep from * to end.

Row 9: Knit.

Rows 10 and 14: [P2, k2] twice, p2, *p10, [k2, p2] twice; rep from * to end.

Rows 11 and 15: *[K2, p2] twice, k2, p8; rep from *, ending [k2, p2] twice, k2.

Rows 12 and 16: [P2, k2] twice, p2, *k8, [p2, k2] twice, p2; rep from * to end.

Rows 13 and 17: *[K2, p2] twice, k10; rep from *, ending [k2, p2] twice, k2.

Row 18: Purl.

Rep rows 1–18 for big basketweave.

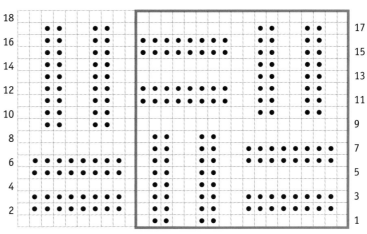

Tumbling Blocks

This is a knit version of the well-known quilt pattern. This pattern begins with wrong side row.

Cast on a multiple of 10 sts.

Row 1 (WS): *[P1, k1] 5 times; rep from * to end.

Row 2: *P2, [k1, p1] 3 times, k2; rep from * to end.

Row 3: *P3, [k1, p1] twice, k3; rep from * to end.

Row 4: *P4, k1, p1, k4; rep from * end.

Row 5: *P5, k5; rep from * to end.

Row 6: *P5, k5; rep from * to end.

Row 7: *K1, p4, k1, p1; rep from * to end.

Row 8: *P1, k1, p3, k3, p1, k1; rep from * to end.

Row 9: *K1, p1, k1, p2, k2, p1, k1, p1; rep from * to end.

Row 10: *[P1, k1] 5 times; rep from * to end.

Row 11: *[K1, p1] 5 times; rep from * to end.

Row 12: *[P1, k1] twice, k1, p2, k1, p1, k1; rep from * to end.

Row 13: *K1, p1, k3, p3, k1, p1; rep from * to end.

Row 14: *P1, k4, p4, k1; rep from * to end.

Row 15: *K5, p5; rep from * to end.

Row 16: *K5, p5; rep from * to end.

Row 17: *K4, p1, k1, p4; rep from * to end.

Row 18: *K3, [p1, k1] twice, p3; rep from * to end.

Row 19: *K2, [p1, k1] 3 times, p2; rep from * to end.

Row 20: *[K1, p1] 5 times; rep from * to end.

Rep rows 1–20 for tumbling blocks.

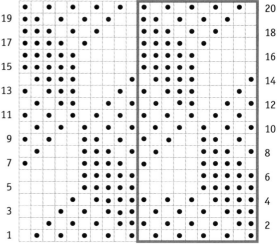

Ruching I

You need two sets of needles for ruching: one suited to your yarn's thickness and a second pair that is one or two sizes larger. A fine, delicate yarn complements this pattern superbly. Start with the smaller needles and the number of stitches required for your desired width. Your stitch count will nearly double for rows 7–14.

Cast on any number of sts.

Rows 1, 3, and 5 (RS): Knit.

Rows 2, 4, and 6: Purl.

Row 7: Change to larger needles. K1, *kfb; rep from * to last st, k1.

Rows 8, 10, 12, and 14: Purl.

Rows 9, 11, and 13: Knit.

Row 15: Change back to smaller needles. K1, *k2tog; rep from * to last st, k1.

Row 16: Purl.

Rep rows 1–16 for ruching I.

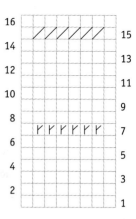

Ruching II

You need two pairs of needles, one suited to your yarn's thickness and one smaller pair. This version begins with the puckered band, creating a ruffle. Begin with the larger needles and cast on twice the number of stitches you need for your final width.

Cast on an even number of sts.

Rows 1, 3, and 5 (RS): Knit.

Rows 2, 4, and 6: Purl.

Row 7: Change to smaller needles. *K2tog; rep from * to end. You'll have half the number of sts you began with.

Rows 8–12: Knit.

Row 13: Change to larger needles. *Kfb; rep from * to end. You'll have the number of sts you began with.

Row 14: Purl.

Rep rows 1–14 for ruching II.

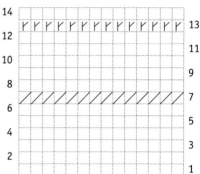

Spirals

Alternating a double increase with a double decrease makes these spiraling cable look-alikes.

Cast on a multiple of 5 sts plus 4.

Row 1 (RS): *P4, knit into front, back, and front of next st; rep from * to last 4 sts, p4.

Row 2: K4, *p3, k4; rep from * to end.

Row 3: *P4, k3tog; rep from * to last 4 sts, p4.

Row 4: K4, *p1, k4; rep from * to end.

Rep rows 1–4 for spirals.

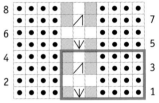

Diagonal Weave

This big pattern looks like ribbons threaded in and out of the background fabric. It's reversible, too.

Cast on a multiple of 16 sts.

Rows 1 and 3 (RS): *K5, p11; rep from * to end.

Row 2: *K11, p5; rep from * to end.

Rows 4 and 6: Purl.

Row 5: Knit.

Rows 7 and 9: *P4, k5, p7; rep from * to end.

Row 8: *K7, p5, k4; rep from * to end.

Rows 10 and 12: Purl.

Row 11: Knit.

Rows 13 and 15: *P8, k5, p3; rep from * to end.

Row 14: *K3, p5, k8; rep from * to end.

Rows 16 and 18: Purl.

Rows 17: Knit.

Rows 19 and 20: *K1, p11, k4; rep from * to end.

Row 20: P4, *k11, p1; rep from * to end.

Rows 22 and 24: Purl.

Row 23: Knit.

Rep rows 1–24 for diagonal weave.

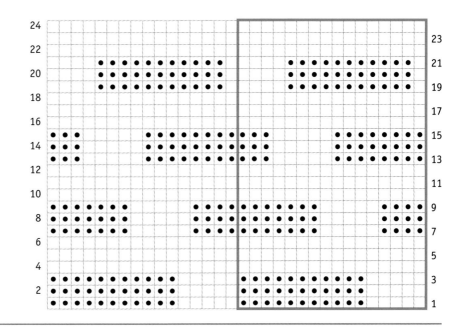

Star Panel

This simple star, a 17-stitch panel, made up of thin lines of purl stitches is lovely centered in cardigan fronts or as a repeating motif on a baby blanket or throw. This pattern begins with a wrong side row.

To use as a single panel, you'll need 17 sts. As a repeating pattern, cast on a multiple of 16 sts plus 1.

Row 1 (WS): K1, p15, k1.

Rows 2, 4, and 18 (RS): Knit.

Rows 3 and 19: K1, [p7, k1] twice.

Rows 5 and 17: K1, p1, [k1, p5, k1] twice, p1, k1.

Rows 6 and 16: K3, p1, k9, p1, k3.

Rows 7 and 15: K1, p3, k1, [p3, k1] twice, p3, k1.

Rows 8 and 14: [K5, p1] twice, k5.

Rows 9 and 13: K1, p5, [k1, p1] twice, k1, p5, k1.

Rows 10 and 12: K7, p1, k1, p1, k7.

Row 11: K1, p1, k5, p1, k1, p1, k5, p1, k1.

Row 20: Knit.

Rep rows 1–20 for star panel.

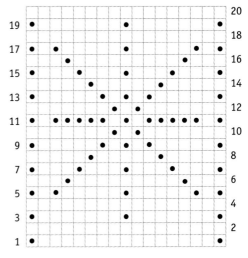

Ribbed Diamonds

This pattern is reversible, so it's great for items where both sides must be seen.

Cast on a multiple of 14 sts plus 1.

Row 1 (RS): *K2, [p1, k1] 6 times; rep from * to last st, k1.

Row 2 and all even-numbered rows (WS): Knit the knit sts and purl the purl sts.

Row 3: *K4, [p1, k1] 4 times, k2; rep from * to last st, k1.

Row 5: *K6, [p1, k1] 2 times, k4; rep from * to last st, k1.

Row 7: *K1, p1, k4, p1, k1, p1, k4, p1; rep from * to last st, k1.

Row 9: *[K1, p1] twice, k7, p1, k1, p1; rep from * to last st, k1.

Row 11: *[K1, p1] 3 times, k3, [p1, k1] twice, p1; rep from * to last st, k1.

Rows 13, 15, 17, and 19: Rep rows 9, 7, 5, and 3, respectively.

Row 20: Rep row 2.

Rep rows 1–20 for ribbed diamonds.

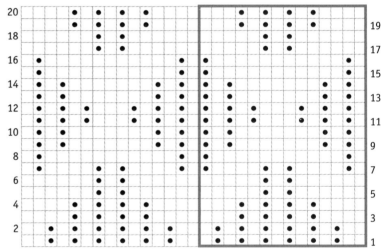

Teepees

Here's an allover pattern that's perfect for throws, wraps, skirts, and other feminine items.

Cast on a multiple of 16 sts.

Row 1 (RS): Knit.

Row 2: *K4, p8, k4; rep from * to end.

Row 3: *P3, k2tog, k3, with left needle, pick up from the back the horizontal strand between last st worked and first st on left needle, and knit into the back and then the front of the picked-up strand, k3, ssk, p3; rep from * to end.

Row 4: *K3, p10, k3; rep from * to end.

Row 5: *P2, k2tog, k3, m1, k2, m1, k3, ssk, p2; rep from * to end.

Row 6: *K2, p12, k2; rep from * to end.

Row 7: *P1, k2tog, k3, m1, k4, m1, k3, ssk, p1; rep from * to end.

Row 8: *K1, p14, k1; rep from * to end.

Row 9: *K2tog, k3, m1, k6, m1, k3, ssk; rep from * to end.

Row 10: Purl.

Rep rows 1–10 for teepees.

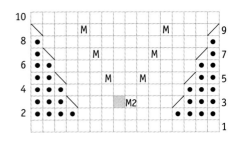

Tic-Tac-Toe

Easy to work and not just for kids, the tic-tac-toe pattern has a unique and playful appeal.

Cast on a multiple of 12 sts plus 3.

Rows 1, 3, 9, and 11 (RS): Knit.

Rows 2, 4, 8, and 10 (WS): Purl.

Rows 5 and 7: *K3, p1, k1, p1, k3, p3; rep from * to last 3 sts, k3.

Row 6: P3, *k1, p1, k1, p4, k1, p4; rep from * to end.

Row 12: P3, *k1, p1, k1, p3, k3, p3; rep from * to end.

Row 13: K3, *p1, k1, p1, k4, p1, k4; rep from * to end.

Row 14: Rep row 12.

Rep rows 1–14 for tic-tac-toe.

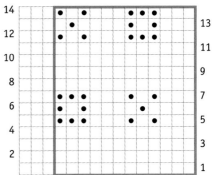

Mock Cable Panel

Here's a knit and purl reproduction of the classic diamond cable pattern.

Cast on 19 sts.

Row 1 (RS): K2, p6, k3, p6, k2.

Row 2 and all even-numbered rows (WS): Knit the knit sts and purl the purl sts.

Row 3: K2, p5, k5, p5, k2.

Row 5: K2, p4, k3, p1, k3, p4, k2.

Row 7: K2, p3, k3, p1, k1, p1, k3, p3, k2.

Row 9: K2, p2, k3, [p1, k1] twice, p1, k3, p2, k2.

Row 11: K2, p1, k3, [p1, k1] 3 times, p1, k3, p1, k2.

Row 13: K5, [p1, k1] 4 times, p1, k5.

Rows 15, 17, 19, 21, and 23: Rep rows 11, 9, 7, 5, and 3, respectively.

Row 24: Rep row 2.

Rep rows 1–24 for mock cable panel.

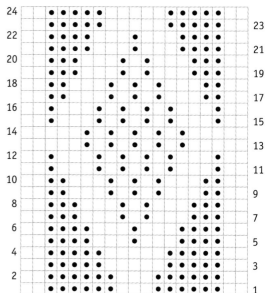

Manhole Cover

Use this playful pattern for scarves, sweaters, bags, or baby blankets.

Cast on a multiple of 8 sts plus 2.

Row 1 (RS): *K2, p3, k2, p1; rep from * to last 2 sts, k2.

Row 2 (WS): P1, *k3, p2, k1, p2; rep from * to last st, k1.

Row 3: P2, *k5, p3; rep from * to end.

Row 4: K2, *p5, k3; rep from * to end.

Row 5: K1, *p3, k2, p1, k2; rep from * to last st, p1.

Row 6: P2, *k3, p2, k1, p2; rep from * to end.

Row 7: K4, p3, *k5, p3; rep from * to last 3 sts, k3.

Row 8: P4, k3, *p5, k3; rep from * to last 3 sts, p3.

Rep rows 1–8 for manhole cover.

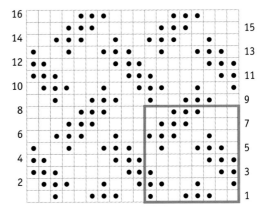

Terrazzo

This big and bold design is also beautiful in a stranded two-color pattern.

Cast on a multiple of 20 sts plus 1.

Row 1 (RS): Purl.

Rows 2 and 16: *K1, [p2, k1] twice, p10, k1, p2; rep from * to last st, k1.

Rows 3, 17 and 19: *P1, k2, p1, k10, [p1, k2] twice; rep from * to last st, p1.

Row 4: *K7, p3, k4, p3, k3; rep from * to last st, k1.

Rows 5, 7 and 13: *P1, k6, p1, k2, p1, k6, p1, k2; rep from * to last st, p1.

Rows 6, 12 and 14: *K1, p2, k1, p6, k1, p2, k1, p6; rep from * to last st, k1.

Row 8: *K1, p2, k1, p2, k5, p2, k5, p2; rep from * to last st, k1.

Row 9: *P1, k2, p1, k4, p2, k4, p1, k2, p1, k2; rep from * to last st, p1.

Row 10: *K1, [p2, k1] twice, p4, k2, p4, k1, p2; rep from * to last st, k1.

Row 11: *P1, k2, p5, k2, p5, k2, p1, k2; rep from * to last st, p1.

Row 15: *[P4, k3] twice, p6; rep from * to last st, p1.

Row 18: Knit.

Row 20: *[K1, p2] twice, k1, p10, k1, p2; rep from * to last st, k1.

Rep rows 1–20 for terrazzo.

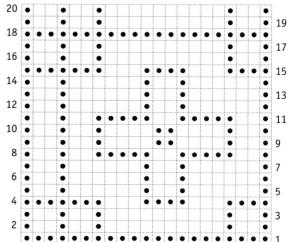

Chevrons

There are an infinite number of chevron patterns. This version is a classic.

Cast on a multiple of 8 sts plus 1.

Row 1 (RS): P1, *k7, p1; rep from * to end.

Row 2: K1, *p7, k1; rep from * to end.

Rows 3 and 12: P2, *k5, p3; rep from *, ending last rep k5, p2.

Rows 4 and 11: K2, *p5, k3; rep from *, ending last rep p5, k2.

Rows 5 and 14: P3, *k3, p5; rep from *, ending last rep k3, p3.

Rows 6 and 13: K3, *p3, k5; rep from *, ending last rep p3, k3.

Row 7: P4, *k1, p7; rep from *, ending last rep k1, p4.

Rows 8 and 15: K4, *p1, k7; rep from *, ending last rep p1, k4.

Row 9: Rep row 2.

Row 10: Rep row 1.

Row 16: Rep row 7.

Rep rows 1–16 for chevrons.

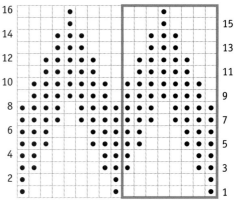

Framed Squares

This geometric pattern lends a modern feel to suits, bags, and skirts.

Cast on a multiple of 10 sts plus 2.

Row 1 (RS): Knit.

Row 2: Purl.

Rows 3 and 11: K2, *p8, k2; rep from * to end.

Row 4: P2, *k8, p2; rep from * to end.

Rows 5, 7, and 9: K2, *p2, k4, p2, k2; rep from * to end.

Rows 6, 8, and 10: P2, *k2, p4, k2, p2; rep from * to end.

Row 12: P2, *k8, p2; rep from * to end.

Rep rows 1–12 for framed squares.

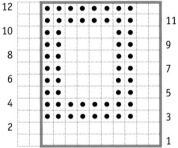

Mini Checks

This simple but pretty pattern is reminiscent of simple seed stitch.

Cast on a multiple of 8 sts.

Rows 1 and 5 (RS): Knit.

Row 2: *P6, k2; rep from * to end.

Rows 3 and 7: Knit the knit sts and purl the purl sts.

Row 4: Purl.

Row 6: P2, *k2, p6; rep from * to last 6 sts, k2, p4.

Row 8: Purl.

Rep rows 1–8 for mini checks.

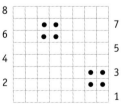

Ladder Stitch

Ladder stitch works wonderfully for blankets, jackets, pullovers, and much more. It's extra easy to work, yet distinctive in appearance.

Cast on a multiple of 8 sts plus 1.

Rows 1 and 3 (RS): *K5, sl 3 pwise wyif; rep from * to last st, k1.

Row 2: P1, *sl 3 pwise wyib, p5; rep from * to end.

Row 4: Purl.

Rows 5 and 7: K1, *sl 3 pwise wyif, k5; rep from * to end.

Row 6: *P5, sl 3 pwise wyib; rep from * to last st, p1.

Row 8: Purl.

Rep rows 1–8 for ladder stitch.

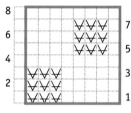

⋁ Sl 1 st pwise with yarn held to RS of work

German Herringbone

This gorgeous pattern, with its many angles and textures, is worked over only six rows, so you'll know it by heart in no time.

Cast on a multiple of 15 sts plus 2.

Row 1 (RS): P2, *m1, k3, p2, p3tog, p2, k3, m1, p2; rep from * to end.

Row 2: *K2, p4, k5, p4; rep from * to last 2 sts, k2.

Row 3: P2, *m1, k4, p1, p3tog, p1, k4, m1, p2; rep from * to end.

Row 4: *K2, p5, k3, p5; rep from * to last 2 sts, k2.

Row 5: P2, *m1, k5, p3tog, k5, m1, p2; rep from * to end.

Row 6: *K2, p6, k1, p6; rep from * to last 2 sts, k2.

Rep rows 1–6 for German herringbone.

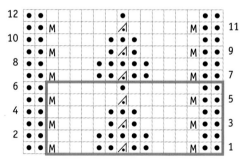

Waffle Stitch

Waffle stitch can be used both as an allover pattern and as a ribbing.

Cast on a multiple of 3 sts.

Rows 1 and 3 (RS): *K2, p1; rep from * to end.

Row 2 (WS): *K1, p2; rep from * to end.

Row 4: Knit.

Rep rows 1–4 for waffle stitch.

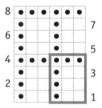

Knit and Purl Plaid

This easy-to-work stitch pattern is perfect for cardigans and fall coats.

Cast on a multiple of 4 sts.

Rows 1 and 2: *K2, p2; rep from * to end.

Row 3: Knit.

Row 4: Purl.

Rows 5 and 6: *K2, p2; rep from * to end.

Row 7: Purl.

Row 8: Knit.

Rep rows 1–8 for knit and purl plaid.

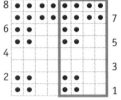

Thatched Weave

This busy pattern looks almost three-dimensional, and it's reversible.

Cast on a multiple of 18 sts.

Row 1 (RS): *K2, p1, k5, p7, k3; rep from * to end.

Row 2 and all even-numbered rows (WS): Knit the knit sts and purl the purl sts.

Row 3: *[K1, p1] twice, k5, p5, k4; rep from * to end.

Row 5: *P1, k3, p1, k5, p3, k5; rep from * to end.

Row 7: *K5, p1, k5, p7; rep from * to end.

Row 9: *[P1, k5] twice, p5, k1; rep from * to end.

Row 11: *K1, [p1, k5] twice, p3, k2; rep from * to end.

Row 13: K2, *p1, k5; rep from * to last 4 sts, p1, k3.

Row 15: *K3, p1, k5, p1, k3, p1, k1, p1, k2; rep from * to end.

Row 17: *K4, p1, k5, p1, k1, p1, k3, p1, k1; rep from * to end.

Row 19: *K5, p7, k5, p1; rep from * to end.

Row 21: *P1, k5, p5, k5, p1, k1; rep from * to end.

Row 23: *K1, p1, k5, p3, k5, p1, k2; rep from * to end.

Row 25: *K2, p7, k5, p1, k3; rep from * to end.

Row 27: *K1, p1, k1, p5, k5, p1, k4; rep from * to end.

Row 29: *P1, k3, p3, k5, p1, k5; rep from * to end.

Row 31: *K5, p1; rep from * to end.

Row 33: *K4, p1, k1, p1, k3, p1, k5, p1, k1; rep from * to end.

Row 35: *[K3, p1] twice, k1, p1, k5, p1, k2; rep from * to end.

Row 36: Rep row 2.

Rep rows 1–36 for thatched weave.

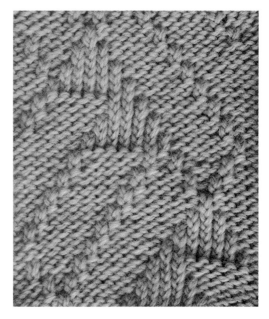

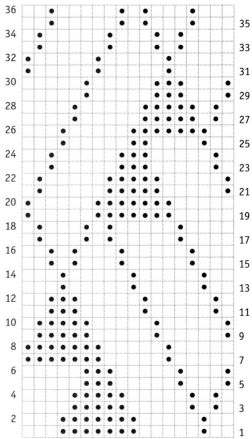

Broken Diagonals

Broken diagonals is a 42-row repeat, so it's good for large or long knits, like throws, wraps, scarves, skirts, coats, and oversized pullovers.

Cast on a multiple of 14 sts.

Row 1 (RS): *P3, k1, p1, k3, p3, k3; rep from * to end.

Row 2 (WS): *K1, p3, k3, [p1, k1] twice, p1, k2; rep from * to end.

Row 3: *P1, k3, p1, k1, p3, k3, p2; rep from * to end.

Row 4: *K3, p3, k1, p1, k3, p3; rep from * to end.

Row 5: *K2, p3, [k1, p1] twice, k1, p3, k1; rep from * to end.

Row 6: *P2, k3, p1, k1, p3, k3, p1; rep from * to end.

Row 7: *P3, k3, p3, k1, p1, k3; rep from * to end.

Row 8: *[K1, p1] 3 times, k3, p3, k2; rep from * to end.

Row 9: *P1, k3, p3, k3, p1, k1, p2; rep from * to end.

Row 10: *K1, p1, [k3, p3] twice; rep from * to end.

Row 11: *P1, k1, p3, k3, p3, k1, p1, k1; rep from * to end.

Row 12: *K1, [p3, k3] twice, p1; rep from * to end.

Row 13: *P1, k1, p1, k3, p3, k3, p2; rep from * to end.

Row 14: *K3, p3, k3, [p1, k1] twice, p1; rep from * to end.

Row 15: *K2, p1, k1, p3, k3, p3, k1; rep from * to end.

Row 16: *P2, k3, p3, k1, p1, k3, p1; rep from * to end.

Row 17: *P3, [k1, p1] twice, k1, p3, k3; rep from * to end.

Row 18: *K1, p3, k3, p1, k1, p3, k2; rep from * to end.

Row 19: *P1, k3, p3, k1, p1, k3, p2; rep from * to end.

Row 20: *K3, [p1, k1] twice, p1, k3, p3; rep from * to end.

Row 21: *K2, p3, k3, p1, k1, p3, k1; rep from * to end.

Row 22: *P2, k1, p1, k3, p3, k3, p1; rep from * to end.

Row 23: *P3, k3, p3, [k1, p1] twice, k1; rep from * to end.

Row 24: *K1, p1, k1, p3, k3, p3, k2; rep from * to end.

Row 25: *P1, [k3, p3] twice, k1; rep from * to end.

Row 26: *K1, p1, k3, p3, k3, p1, k1, p1; rep from * to end.

Row 27: *P1, k1, [p3, k3] twice; rep from * to end.

Row 28: *K1, p3, k3, p3, k1, p1, k2; rep from * to end.

Row 29: *[P1, k1] 3 times, p3, k3, p2; rep from * to end.

Row 30: *K3, p3, k3, p1, k1, p3; rep from * to end.

Row 31: *K2, p3, k1, p1, k3, p3, k1; rep from * to end.

Row 32: *P2, k3, [p1, k1] twice, p1, k3, p1; rep from * to end.

Row 33: *P3, k3, p1, k1, p3, k3; rep from * to end.

Row 34: *K1, p3, k1, p1, k3, p3, k2; rep from * to end.

Row 35: *P1, k3, p3, [k1, p1] twice, k1, p2; rep from * to end.

Row 36: *K3, p1, k1, p3, k3, p3; rep from * to end.

Row 37: *K2, p3, k3, p3, k1, p1, k1; rep from * to end.

Row 38: *[K1, p1] twice, k3, p3, k3, p1; rep from * to end.

Row 39: *[P3, k3] twice, p1, k1; rep from * to end.

Row 40: *[K3, p3] twice, k1, p1; rep from * to end.

Row 41: *[P1, k1] twice, p3, k3, p3, k1; rep from * to end.

Row 42: *P2, k3, p3, k3, p1, k1, p1; rep from * to end.

Rep rows 1–42 for broken diagonals.

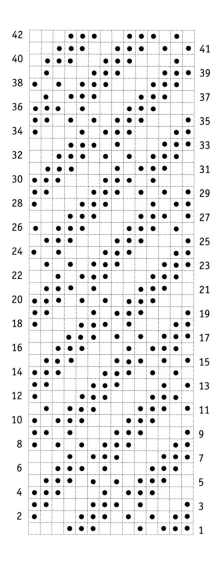

Circles

This bold circular pattern with its modern style works wonderfully for fall jackets, cushion covers, straight skirts, and bright baby blankets. Circles is reversible, too. The chart shows circular motifs in reverse stockinette stitch, and the photo shows the reverse.

Cast on a multiple of 14 sts plus 1.

Row 1 (WS): *P3, k9, p2; rep from * to last st, p1.

Row 2 (RS): *K2, p3, k5, p3, k1; rep from * to last st, k1.

Rows 3 and 13: *P1, k3, p7, k3; rep from * to last st, p1.

Rows 4 and 12: *P3, k9, p2; rep from * to last st, p1.

Rows 5 and 11: *K2, p11, k1; rep from * to last st, k1.

Rows 6, 8, and 10: *P1, k4, p5, k4; rep from * to last st, p1.

Rows 7 and 9: *K1, p4, k5, p4; rep from * to last st, k1.

Row 14: Rep row 2.

Rep rows 1–14 for circles; when finished lengthwise, complete the pattern with a row 1.

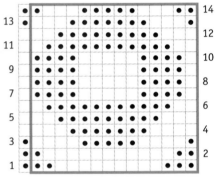

Celtic Design

This pattern requires a bit more concentration, but the end result is worth it.

Cast on a multiple of 16 sts plus 1.

Row 1 (RS): *[K1, p1] 3 times, [k2, p1] twice, [k1, p1] twice; rep from * to last st, k1.

Rows 2 and 8 (WS): *P2, k1, p1, k1, p7, [k1, p1] twice; rep from * to last st, p1.

Rows 3 and 7: *P1, k2, p1, k1, p1, [k2, p1] twice, k1, p1, k2; rep from * to last st, p1.

Row 4: *K2, p2, k1, p7, k1, p2, k1; rep from * to last st, k1.

Row 5: *P3, [k2, p1] 3 times, k2, p2; rep from * to last st, p1.

Row 6: *K2, p2, k1, p7, k1, p2, k1; rep from * to last st, k1.

Row 9: *K3, p1, k1, p1, [k2, p1] twice, k1, p1, k2; rep from * to last st, k1.

Row 10: *P4, k1, p7, k1, p3; rep from * to last st, p1.

Row 11: *[K2, p1] 5 times, k1; rep from * to last st, k1.

Row 12: *[P1, k1] twice, p2, k1, p3, k1, p2, k1, p1, k1; rep from * to last st, p1.

Row 13: *[P1, k1] twice, [p1, k3] twice, [p1, k1] twice; rep from * to last st, p1.

Row 14: *P1, k1, p3, k1, p5, k1, p3, k1; rep from * to last st, p1.

Row 15: *[P1, k2] twice, [p1, k1] twice, [p1, k2] twice; rep from * to last st, p1.

Row 16: *[P2, k1, p1, k1] 3 times, p1; rep from * to last st, p1.

Rep rows 1–16 for Celtic pattern; when finished lengthwise, complete the pattern with a row 1.

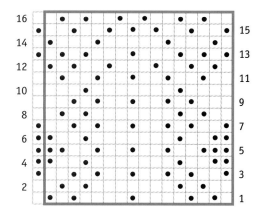

Concentric Diamonds

This 16-stitch, 16-row repeat works well as a border or as an allover pattern on pullovers, skirts, and scarves. Both sides are equally appealing.

Cast on a multiple of 16 sts plus 1.

Rows 1, 7, and 11 (RS): *[K2, p1] 5 times, k1; rep from *, ending last rep k2.

Rows 2, 8, and 10 (WS): P1, *[k1, p2] twice, k1, p1; rep from * to end.

Rows 3, 9, and 15: *P1, [k2, p1] twice, k3, [p1, k2] twice; rep from * to last st, p1.

Rows 4 and 14: *[P2, k1] 5 times, p1; rep from *, ending last rep p2.

Rows 5 and 13: *K1, [p1, k2] twice, p1; rep from * to last st, k1.

Rows 6 and 12: *K1, [p1, k2] twice, p1; rep from * to last st, k1.

Row 16: Rep row 2.

Rep rows 1–16 for concentric diamonds; when finished lengthwise, complete the pattern with a row 1.

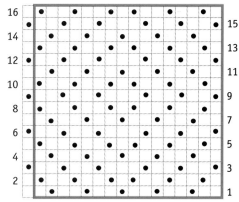

Diamond Panel

This simple 21-stitch panel can be worked as part of a larger combination of panels and stitch patterns or used by itself centered on a pullover, cushion cover, or cardigan fronts. This is another reversible panel. The chart shows the diamond motifs on a ground of reverse stockinette stitch, and the photo shows the reverse.

Row 1 (RS): K2, p1, k3, p9, k3, p1, k2.

Rows 2: P2, k2, p3, k7, p3, k2, p2.

Rows 3 and 11: K2, p3, k3, p5, k3, p3, k2.

Rows 4 and 10: P2, k4, p3, k3, p3, k4, p2.

Rows 5 and 9: K2, p5, k3, p1, k3, p5, k2.

Rows 6 and 8: P2, k6, p5, k6, p2.

Row 7: K2, p7, k3, p7, k2.

Row 12: Rep row 2.

Rep rows 1–12 for diamond panel.

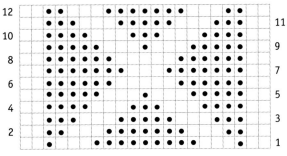

Chains

Here is another eye-catching reversible pattern that is easy to work.

Cast on a multiple of 6 sts.

Row 1 (RS): *K1, p1, k1, p3; rep from * to end.

Row 2 (WS): *[K1, p1] 3 times; rep from * to end.

Row 3: *K1, p1, k1, p3; rep from * to end.

Row 4: *P1, k1, p1, k3; rep from * to end.

Row 5: *[P1, k1] 3 times; rep from * to end.

Row 6: *P1, k1, p1, k3; rep from * to end.

Rep rows 1–6 for chains.

Seed Stitch Flags

Alternating stockinette stitch triangles with seed stitch triangles lends subtlety to this geometric pattern.

Cast on a multiple of 16 sts.

Row 1 (RS): *P1, k7, [p1, k1] 4 times; rep from * to end.

Row 2 (WS): *P2, [k1, p1] 3 times, p6, k1, p1; rep from * to end.

Rows 3 and 11: *P1, k1, p1, k5, [p1, k1] twice, p1, k3; rep from * to end.

Rows 4 and 10: *P4, [k1, p1] twice; rep from * to end.

Rows 5 and 9: *P1, [k1, p1] twice, k3, p1, k1, p1, k5; rep from * to end.

Rows 6 and 8: *P6, k1, p3, [k1, p1] 3 times; rep from * to end.

Row 7: *P1, [k1, p1] 4 times, k7; rep from * to end.

Row 12: Rep row 2.

Rep rows 1–12 for seed stitch flags.

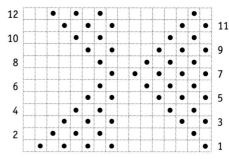

Garlands

This design, with its fluid waves, opposes the usual geometric knit and purl patterns.

Cast on a multiple of 13 sts plus 4.

Row 1 (RS): P4, *k9, p4; rep from * to end.

Row 2 (WS): K6, *p5, k8; rep from * to last 11 sts, p5, k6.

Row 3: P7, *k3, p10; rep from * to last 10 sts, k3, p7.

Row 4: K8, *p1, k12; rep from * to last 9 sts, p1, k8.

Row 5: K4, *p9, k4; rep from * to end.

Row 6: P6, *k5, p8; rep from * to last 11 sts, k5, p6.

Row 7: K7, *p3, k10; rep from * to last 10 sts, p3, k7.

Row 8: P8, *k1, p12; rep from * to last 9 sts, k1, p8.

Row 9: Knit.

Row 10: Purl.

Rep rows 1–10 for garlands.

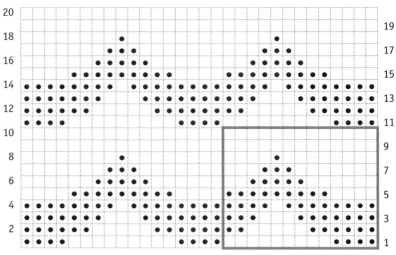

CHAPTER 2

Rib Patterns

1 x 1 Rib

This is the most basic rib. A reversible pattern, you often see it on cuffs, hems, and necklines.

Cast on an odd number of sts.

Row 1 (RS): K1, *p1, k1; rep from * to end.

Row 2 (WS): P1, *k1, p1; rep from * to end.

Rep rows 1 and 2 for 1 x 1 rib.

2 x 2 Rib

This easy pattern lies flat and looks the same on both sides.

Cast on a multiple of 4 sts plus 2.

Row 1 (RS): K2, *p2, k2; rep from * to end.

Row 2 (WS): P2, *k2, p2; rep from * to end.

Rep rows 1 and 2 for 2 x 2 rib.

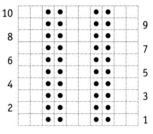

Wide Rib

Another basic rib variation, this wide rib works well on cuffs and hems or as an allover pattern on fitted sweaters.

Cast on a multiple of 7 sts plus 2.

Row 1 (RS): P2, *k5, p2; rep from * to end.

Row 2 (WS): K2, *p5, k2; rep from * to end.

Rep rows 1 and 2 for wide rib.

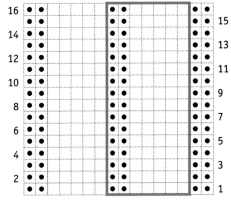

Garter Rib I

This easy pattern lies flat and looks the same on both sides.

Cast on a multiple of 4 sts plus 2.

Row 1: K2, *p2, k2; rep from * to end.

Rep row 1 for garter rib I.

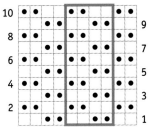

Garter Rib II

This pattern blends garter stitch and stockinette stitch to form the rib, rather than the traditional stockinette stitch–reverse stockinette stitch combination.

Cast on a multiple of 8 sts plus 4.

Row 1 (RS): Knit.

Row 2 (WS): P4, *k4, p4; rep from * to end.

Rep rows 1 and 2 for garter rib II.

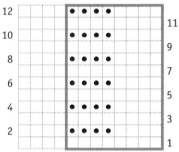

Broken Rib

This easy two-row pattern looks very different on the front and on the back but is attractive on both sides.

Cast on an odd number of sts.

Row 1 (RS): Knit.

Row 2 (WS): P1, *k1, p1; rep from * to end.

Rep rows 1 and 2 for broken rib.

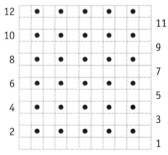

Rib-and-Ridge Stitch

This rib is not elastic, so it works best as an allover design. The right side looks like a rippled 1 x 1 rib, and the wrong side looks like an interrupted rib.

Cast on a multiple of 2 sts plus 1.

Row 1 (RS): Knit.

Row 2 (WS): Purl.

Row 3: P1, *k1, p1; rep from * to end.

Row 4: K1, *p1, k1; rep from * to end.

Rep rows 1–4 for rib-and-ridge stitch.

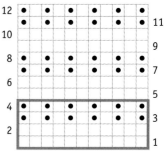

Seeded Rib

A seeded rib pattern is very attractive, and it results in a highly textured fabric.

Cast on a multiple of 4 sts plus 1.

Row 1 (RS): P1, *k3, p1; rep from * to end.

Row 2 (WS): K2, p1, *k3, p1; rep from * to last 2 sts, k2.

Rep rows 1 and 2 for seeded rib.

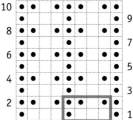

Twisted Rib

For twisted rib, you knit stitches through the back loops on right-side rows.

Cast on an odd number of sts.

Row 1 (RS): K1 tbl, *p1, k1 tbl; rep from * to end.

Row 2 (WS): P1, *k1, p1; rep from * to end.

Rep rows 1 and 2 for twisted rib.

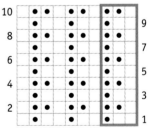

Farrow Rib

Farrow rib looks the same on both sides, so it is perfect for scarves, shawls, and throws.

Cast on a multiple of 3 sts plus 1.

Row 1 (RS): *K2, p1; rep from * to last st, k1.

Row 2 (WS): P1, *k2, p1; rep from * to end.

Rep rows 1 and 2 for farrow rib.

Twin Rib

Twin rib looks the same on both sides, even though the two rows that make up the pattern are different. It is good for just about anything—from jackets, sweaters, and dresses to scarves and bags.

Cast on a multiple of 6 sts.

Row 1 (RS): *K3, p3; rep from * to end.

Row 2 (WS): *K1, p1; rep from * to end.

Rep rows 1 and 2 for twin rib.

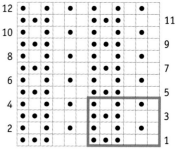

Alternating Dotted Rib

This stitch works well as an allover pattern. It looks like a rib but doesn't pull in as much as a traditional rib.

Cast on a multiple of 4 sts plus 3.

Row 1 (RS): K1, *p1, k3; rep from * to last 2 sts, p1, k1.

Row 2 (WS): Purl.

Row 3: K3, *p1, k3; rep from * to end.

Row 4: Purl.

Rep rows 1–4 for alternating dotted rib.

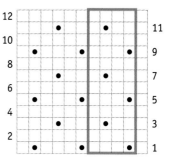

Piqué Rib

Piqué rib is an eye-catching pattern that works for sweaters, socks, hats, and more.

Cast on a multiple of 10 sts.

Rows 1 and 3 (RS): *P3, k1, p3, k3; rep from * to end.

Row 2 (WS): *P3, k3, p1, k3; rep from * to end.

Row 4: Knit.

Rep rows 1–4 for piqué rib.

Rickrack Rib

This is a very pretty, busy pattern that looks great on vintage-style sweaters.

Cast on a multiple of 3 sts plus 1.

Row 1 (RS): K1 tbl, *yo, k2tog tbl, k1 tbl; rep from * to end.

Row 2 (WS): P1 tbl, *p2, p1 tbl; rep from * to end.

Row 3: K1 tbl, *k2tog, yo, k1 tbl; rep from * to end.

Row 4: P1 tbl, *p2, p1 tbl; rep from * to end.

Rep rows 1–4 for rickrack rib.

Bobble Rib

Bobble rib adds an elegant touch to cuffs and hems; it's also great for close-fitting sleeves and pullovers.

5-st bobble: Knit into front, back, front, back, and front of stitch. Then, without turning, pass 4th st over 5th st and off, 3rd st over 5th and off, 2nd st over 5th and off, and 1st st over 5th and off.

Cast on a multiple of 8 sts plus 3.

Row 1 (RS): *K3, p2, make 5-st bobble, p2; rep from * to last 3 sts, k3.

Row 2 (WS): P3, *k2, p1, k2, p3; rep from * to end.

Row 3: *K3, p5; rep from * to last 3 sts, k3.

Row 4: P3, *k2, p1, k2, p3; rep from * to end.

Rep rows 1–4 for bobble rib.

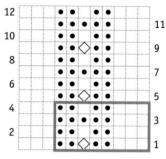

Bell Rib

This beautiful pattern makes an exciting edging for a woman's sweater. It also works well as an allover pattern.

Cast on a multiple of 5 sts plus 2.

Rows 1 and 3 (RS): P2, *k3, p2; rep from * to end.

Rows 2 and 4 (WS): K2, *p3, k2; rep from * to end.

Row 5: P2, *yo, sk2p, yo, p2; rep from * to end.

Row 6: K2, *p3, k2; rep from * to end.

Rep rows 1–6 for bell rib.

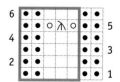

Undulating Rib

This pattern is worked like a 2 x 2 rib, but the addition of twisted stitches and yarn overs gives it a cabled look. This pattern begins with a wrong side row.

Cast on a multiple of 4 sts plus 2.

Row 1 (WS): K2, *p2, k2; rep from * to end.

Row 2 (RS): P2, *[k2tog tbl, then knit same 2 sts tog through front loops], p2; rep from * to end.

Row 3: K2, *p1, yo, p1, k2; rep from * to end.

Row 4: P2, *sl 1, k1, psso, k1, p2; rep from * to end.

Rep rows 1–4 for undulating rib.

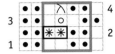

Pleated Rib

By alternating narrow rib with wide rib, this ingenious pattern forms lovely pleats. Take care not to flatten the pleats when blocking. This pattern looks the same on both sides, so there is no right or wrong side.

Cast on a multiple of 13 sts.

Row 1: *K4, [p1, k1] 3 times, p3; rep from * to end.

Row 2: *K3, [p1, k1] 3 times, p4; rep from * to end.

Rep rows 1 and 2 for pleated rib.

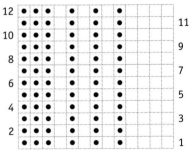

Diagonal Rib

Diagonal rib is a pattern that can be used not only as a decorative border but also as an allover pattern.

Cast on a multiple of 4 sts.

Row 1 (RS): *K2, p2; rep from * to end.

Row 2 (WS): Rep row 1.

Row 3: K1, *p2, k2; rep from * to last 3 sts, p2, k1.

Row 4: P1, *k2, p2; rep from * to last 3 sts, k2, p1.

Row 5: *P2, k2; rep from * to end.

Row 6: Rep row 5.

Row 7: Rep row 4.

Row 8: Rep row 3.

Rep rows 1–8 for diagonal rib.

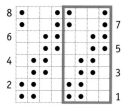

Wavy Rib

Add a touch of fun to socks, mittens, and cuffs with wavy rib.

Cast on a multiple of 6 sts.

Rows 1, 3, and 5 (RS): *P4, k2; rep from * to end.

Rows 2, 4, and 6 (WS): *P2, k4; rep from * to end.

Row 7: *P2, sl 2 sts to cn and hold at back of work, k2, p2 from cn; rep from * to end.

Rows 8, 10, and 12: K2, *p2, k4; rep from * to last 4 sts, p2, k2.

Rows 9 and 11: P2, *k2, p4; rep from * to last 4 sts, k2, p2.

Row 13: *Sl 2 sts to cn and hold at back of work, k2, p2 from cn, p2; rep from * to end.

Rows 14, 16, and 18: *K4, p2; rep from * to end.

Rows 15 and 17: *K2, p4; rep from * to end.

Row 19: P4, *sl 2 sts to cn, k2, p2 from cn, p2; rep from * to last 2 sts, k2.

Rep rows 2–19 for wavy rib.

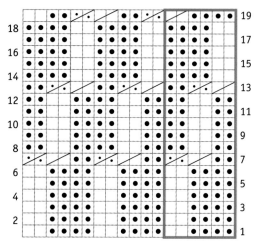

Eyelet Rib

Use eyelet rib to add a delicate touch to baby clothes, socks, and feminine sweaters.

Cast on a multiple of 4 sts.

Rows 1 and 3 (RS): *K1, p3; rep from * to end.

Rows 2 and 4 (WS): *K3, p1; rep from * to end.

Row 5: *K1, p2tog, yo, p1; rep from * to end.

Row 6: *K3, p1; rep from * to end.

Rep rows 1–6 for eyelet rib.

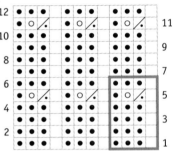

Sloping Rib

This is a form of diagonal rib, but more oblique.

Cast on a multiple of 4 sts.

Row 1 (RS): *K2, p2; rep from * to end.

Row 2 (WS): K1, *p2, k2; rep from * to last 3 sts, p2, k1.

Row 3: *P2, k2; rep from * to end.

Row 4: P1, *k2, p2; rep from * to last 3 sts, k2, p1.

Rep rows 1–4 for sloping rib.

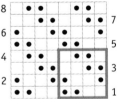

Lacy Rib

Here's a fancy rib that will dress up sweaters, socks, and mitten cuffs. This pattern begins with a wrong side row.

Cast on a multiple of 6 sts plus 2.

Rows 1 and 3 (WS): *P2, k1; rep from * to last 2 sts, p2.

Row 2 (RS): *K2, p1, yo, ssk, p1; rep from * to last 2 sts, k2.

Row 4: *K2, p1, k2tog, yo, p1; rep from * to last 2 sts, k2.

Rep rows 1–4 for lacy rib.

Tweed Rib

This rib is more decorative than elastic. It's perfect for bags, cardigans, bedspreads, and cushions.

Cast on a multiple of 6 sts.

Row 1 (RS): *P3, sl 1 wyif, k1, sl 1 wyif; rep from * to end.

Row 2 (WS): *P3, k3; rep from * to end.

Row 3: *P3, k1, sl 1 wyif, k1; rep from * to end.

Row 4: *P3, k3; rep from * to end.

Rep rows 1–4 for tweed rib.

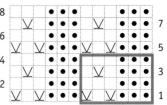

Triangle Rib

This bold pattern is reversible and works perfectly for blankets, tote bags, jackets, and scarves.

Cast on a multiple of 8 sts.

Row 1 (RS): *P1, k7; rep from * to end.

Row 2 (WS): *P6, k2; rep from * to end.

Rows 3 and 11: *P3, k5; rep from * to end.

Rows 4 and 10: *P4, k4; rep from * to end.

Rows 5 and 9: *P5, k3; rep from * to end.

Row 6: *P2, k6; rep from * to end.

Row 7: *P7, k1; rep from * to end.

Row 8: *P2, k6; rep from * to end.

Row 12: *P6, k2; rep from * to end.

Rep rows 1–12 for triangle rib.

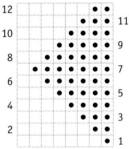

Embossed Rib

You can use this striking textural pattern for bags, jackets, scarves, and pullovers.

Cast on a multiple of 2 sts plus 1.

Row 1 (RS): Knit.

Row 2 (WS): P1, *k1 in st below (insert needle into center of st below next st on left needle and knit it, dropping unworked stitch above off left needle), p1; rep from * to end.

Rep rows 1 and 2 for embossed rib.

Balloon Rib

This is a fun pattern that adds flair to cuffs and hems, but it also can be used as an allover pattern for a highly textured effect.

Cast on a multiple of 3 sts plus 2.

Row 1 (RS): P2, *yo, k1, yo, p2; rep from * to end.

Row 2: K2, *p3, k2; rep from * to end.

Row 3: P2, *k3, p2; rep from * to end.

Row 4: K2, *p3tog, k2; rep from * to end.

Rep rows 1–4 for balloon rib.

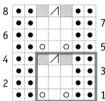

Broken Ripple Rib

This dynamic fabric comes from interrupting the rib horizontally and then jogging the ribs to the left every few rows. This pattern begins with a wrong side row.

Cast on a multiple of 5 sts plus 1.

Row 1 (WS): Knit.

Rows 2 and 4 (RS): *K2, p3; rep from * to last st, k1.

Row 3: P1, *k3, p2; rep from * to end.

Row 5: Knit.

Row 6: P1, *k2, p3; rep from * to end.

Row 7: *K3, p2; rep from * to last st, k1.

Row 8: Rep row 6.

Rep rows 1–8 for broken ripple rib.

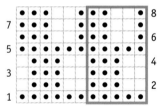

Wrapped Rib

You can transform a plain rib into something special with wrapped stitches.

Cast on a multiple of 18 sts plus 4.

Rows 1, 3, 5, and 7 (RS): K4, *p5, k4; rep from * to end.

Row 2 and all even-numbered rows (WS): P4, *k5, p4; rep from * to end.

Rows 9 and 11: *Cluster 4 (yfwd, sl 4 sts purlwise, ybk, return these 4 sts to left needle and knit them), p5, k4, p5; rep from * to last 4 sts, cluster 4.

Rows 13, 15, 17, and 19: K4, *p5, k4; rep from * to end.

Rows 21 and 23: K4, *p5, cluster 4, p5, k4; rep from * to end.

Row 24: P4, *k5, p4; rep from * to end.

Rep rows 1–24 for wrapped rib.

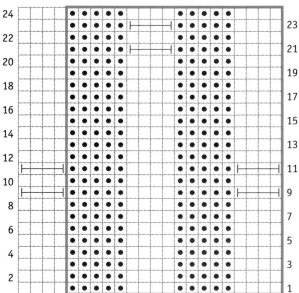

Plaited Rib

Give ribs a woven look by "plaiting" them.

Cast on a multiple of 5 sts plus 2.

Row 1 (RS): P2, *k1, LT, p2; rep from * to end.

Row 2 (WS): K2, *p1, RT, k2; rep from * to end.

NOTE: Be sure to work the wrong-side version of the RT in row 2.

Rep rows 1 and 2 for plaited rib.

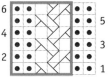

Corded Rib

Repeating the same row on both right and wrong sides results in this delicate ribbing.

Cast on a multiple of 4 sts plus 2.

Row 1: K1, *ssk, m1, p2; rep from * to last st, k1.

Rep row 1 for corded rib.

$\diagdown$ **RS:** ssk

$\diagdown$ **WS:** ssk

Feather Rib

You use a double decrease to create this elegant rib pattern. When working the s2kp decrease, be sure to slip the 2 sts knitwise at the same time. This pattern begins with a wrong side.

Cast on a multiple of 10 sts plus 3.

Row 1 (WS): K3, *p1 tbl, p5, p1 tbl, k3; rep from * to end.

Row 2: P3, *yo, k2, s2kp, k2, yo, p3; rep from * to end.

Rep rows 1 and 2 for feather rib.

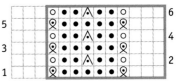

Double-Stitch Rib

This rib looks intricate but is simple to do. It also works wonderfully as an allover pattern.

Cast on an even number of sts, plus 1.

Row 1 (RS): Knit.

Row 2: P1, *k1 in st below (insert needle into center of st below next st on left needle and knit it, dropping unworked st above from left needle at the same time), p1; rep from * to end.

Rep rows 1 and 2 for double-stitch rib.

Diagonal Check Rib

Dress up diagonal rib with a checked pattern inserted between the ribs.

Cast on a multiple of 12 sts.

Row 1 (RS): *P1, k1, p2, k2, p2, k3, p1; rep from * to end.

Row 2 (WS): *K2, p3, k2, p1, k2, p2; rep from * to end.

Row 3: *P2, k2, p2, k3, p2, k1; rep from * to end.

Row 4: *P2, k2, p3, k2, p1, k2; rep from * to end.

Row 5: *K2, p2, k3, p2, k1, p2; rep from * to end.

Row 6: *K2, p2, k2, p3, k2, p1; rep from * to end.

Row 7: *P2, k3, p2, k1, p2, k2; rep from * to end.

Row 8: *K1, p1, k2, p2, k2, p3, k1; rep from * to end.

Row 9: *K3, p2, k1, p2, k2, p2; rep from * to end.

Row 10: *P1, k2, p1, [k2, p2] twice; rep from * to end.

Row 11: *[K1, p2] twice, k2, p2, k2; rep from * to end.

Row 12: *P3, k2, p1, k2, p2, k2; rep from * to end.

Rep rows 1–12 for diagonal check rib.

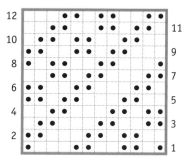

Twist-Stitch Columns

For a looser, open rib, try using a needle two or three sizes larger than your yarn calls for. This pattern begins with a wrong side row.

Cast on a multiple of 6 sts plus 2.

Row 1 (WS): K2, *p4, k2; rep from * to end.

Row 2 (RS): P2, *LT, RT, p2; rep from * to end.

Rep rows 1 and 2 for twist-stitch columns.

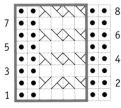

Vacillating Rib

So simple to work, but so eye-catching at the same time.

Cast on a multiple of 8 sts.

Rows 1 and 3 (RS): *K3, sl 1 wyif, k3, p1; rep from * to end.

Row 2 (WS): *K1, p3, sl 1 wyib, p3; rep from * to end.

Row 4: *K1, p3, k1, p3; rep from * to end.

Rep rows 1–4 for vacillating rib.

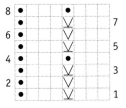

Threaded Rib

This rib works well for borders and as an allover pattern. This pattern is difficult to represent in a chart form, but you won't find it difficult to work.

Cast on a multiple of 6 sts.

Row 1 and all odd-numbered rows (RS): *P2, k1; rep from * to end.

Rows 2, 4, 6, and 8 (WS): *P1, k2, p1, sl 1 wyif, p1, yo, pass sl st over the p1 and the yo; rep from * to end.

Rows 10, 12, 14, and 16: *P1, sl 1 wyif, p1, yo, pass the sl st over the p1 and the yo, p1, k2; rep from * to end.

Rep rows 1–16 for threaded rib.

Slipstitch Rib

The slipped stitches lend a rope-like texture to this rib. This pattern begins with a wrong side row.

Cast on a multiple of 3 sts.

Row 1 (WS): *P2, m1, k1; rep from * to end.

Row 2 (RS): *P1, sl 1, k2, pass the sl st over the 2 knit sts; rep from * to end.

Rep rows 1 and 2 for slipstitch rib.

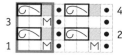

Mock Cable Rib I

Alternating increases with decreases every other row is what gives this rib its cabled look.

Cast on a multiple of 5 sts.

Row 1 (RS): *P4, kfbf; rep from * to end.

Row 2 (WS): *P3, k4; rep from * to end.

Row 3: *P4, k3tog; rep from * to end.

Row 4: *P1, k4; rep from * to end.

Rep rows 1–4 for mock cable rib I.

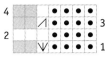

Mock Cable Rib II

For this rib, passing slipped stitches over other stitches creates mock cables.

Cast on a multiple of 8 sts.

Row 1 (RS): *P5, k3; rep from * to end.

Row 2 (WS): *P3, k5; rep from * to end.

Row 3: *P5, sl 1, k2, yo, pass the sl st over the 2 knit sts and the yo; rep from * to end.

Row 4: *P3, k5; rep from * to end.

Rep rows 1–4 for mock cable rib II.

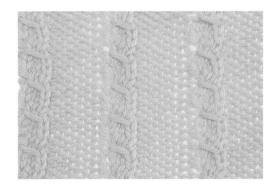

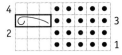

Moss Rib

This rib looks intricate but is simple to do. It also works wonderfully as an allover pattern.

Cast on a multiple of 7 sts plus 3.

Row 1 (RS): P3, *k1, p1, k2, p3; rep from * to end.

Row 2 (WS): K3, *p2, k1, p1, k3; rep from * to end.

Row 3: P3, *k2, p1, k1, p3; rep from * to end.

Row 4: K3, *p1, k1, p2, k3; rep from * to end.

Rep rows 1–4 for moss rib.

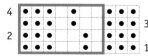

Twisted Eyelet Rib

This pretty rib is perfect for just about anything—edgings, baby clothes, cardigans, and more. Or dress up a plain stockinette-stitch sweater with twisted eyelet rib sleeves.

Cast on a multiple of 5 sts plus 3.

Row 1 (RS): *P1, k1 tbl, p1, k2; rep from * to last 3 sts, p1, k1 tbl, p1.

Row 2 (WS): K1, p1 tbl, k1, *p2, k1, p1 tbl, k1; rep from * to end.

Row 3: *P1, k1 tbl, p1, k1, yo, k1; rep from * to last 3 sts, p1, k1 tbl, p1.

Row 4: K1, p1 tbl, k1, *p3, k1, p1 tbl, k1; rep from * to end.

Row 5: *P1, k1 tbl, p1, k3, pass 3rd st on right needle over first 2 sts; rep from * to last 3 sts, p1, k1 tbl, p1.

Rep rows 2–5 for twisted eyelet rib.

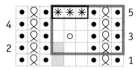

   K3, pass 3rd st on right needle over first 2 sts.

Plaid Rib

More of an allover pattern than an actual rib, this stitch makes beautiful coats, totes, and cushion covers.

Cast on a multiple of 12 sts plus 6.

Rows 1 and 3 (RS): K6, *p6, k6; rep from * to end.

Rows 2 and 4 (WS): *P6, k6; rep from * to to last 6 sts, p6.

Rows 5 and 7: Knit.

Rows 6 and 8: Purl.

Rep rows 1–8 for plaid rib.

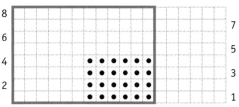

Openwork Rib

This is a feminine and decorative rib. Be sure to stretch and block it to showcase the openwork. This pattern begins with a wrong side row.

Cast on a multiple of 6 sts plus 2.

Row 1 (WS): K2, *p4, k2; rep from * to end.

Row 2 (RS): P2, *k2tog, yo twice, skp, p2; rep from * to end.

Row 3: K2, *p1, purl into the front of the first yo, then purl into the back of the second yo, p1, k2; rep from * to end.

Row 4: P2, *yo, skp, k2tog, yo, p2; rep from * to end.

Rep rows 1–4 for openwork rib.

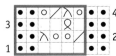

Dotted Rectangle Rib

Use this rib pattern for cuffs, hems, bags, throws, and pillow covers.

Cast on a multiple of 4 sts plus 1.

Rows 1, 5, and 8: *K1, p3; rep from * to last st, k1.

Rows 2, 6, 7, and 11: *P1, k3; rep from * to last st, p1.

Rows 3 and 10: *[K1, p1] twice; rep from * to last st, k1.

Rows 4 and 9: *[P1, k1] twice; rep from * to last st, p1.

Row 12: Work as for row 8.

Rep rows 1–12 for dotted rectangle rib.

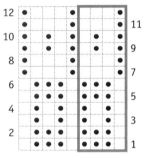

Arrow Rib

This pattern combines eyelet increases with a prominent double decrease to create an elegant rib.

Cast on a multiple of 15 sts plus 2.

Row 1 (RS): *K2, p2, yo, k3, sk2p, k3, yo, p2; rep from * to last 2 sts, k2.

Rows 2, 4, and 6 (WS): *P2, k2, p9, k2; rep from * to last 2 sts, p2.

Row 3: *K2, p2, k1, yo, k2, sk2p, k2, yo, k1, p2; rep from * to last 2 sts, k2.

Row 5: *K2, p2, k2, yo, k1, sk2p, k1, yo, k2, p2; rep from * to last 2 sts, k2.

Row 7: *K2, p2, k3, yo, sk2p, yo, k3, p2; rep from * to last 2 sts, k2.

Row 8: Work as for row 2.

Rep rows 1–8 for arrow rib.

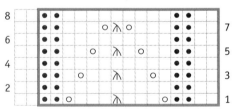

CHAPTER 3

Bobbles and Textured Patterns

Feather and Fan

Feather and fan, also known as old shale or peacock stitch, is an intricate, sumptuous-looking pattern that works up almost effortlessly. For a more finished look, you can add two stitches to each edge as a border; just knit them on both right-side and wrong-side rows.

Cast on a multiple of 18 sts.

Row 1 (RS): Knit.

Row 2 (WS): Purl.

Row 3: *[K2tog] 3 times, [yo, k1] 6 times, [k2tog] 3 times; rep from * to end.

Row 4: Knit.

Rep rows 1–4 for feather and fan.

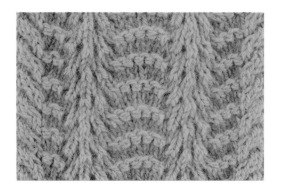

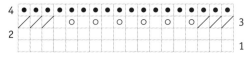

Bobble Stitch

Here's a pattern where you work a series of bobbles on every 6th row.

Mb (make bobble): K1, p1, k1, p1, k1 into next st, turn, p5, turn, k5, pass the 4 sts one at a time over the knit st and off the needle to finish bobble.

Cast on a multiple of 4 sts plus 3.

Row 1 (RS—bobble row): *K3, mb; rep from * to last 3 sts, k3.

Rows 2, 4, and 6 (WS): Purl.

Rows 3 and 5: Knit.

Row 7 (bobble row): K1, mb, *k3, mb; rep from * to last st, k1.

Rows 8 and,10: Purl.

Rows 9 and 11: Knit.

Row 12: Purl.

Rep rows 1–12 for bobble stitch.

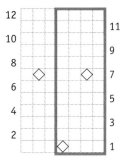

Trinity Stitch

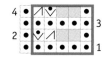

Trinity stitch, also referred to as bramble stitch, works wonderfully for hems, cuffs, collars, and slouchy lined bags, or framing central cable panels on Aran sweaters.

Cast on a multiple of 4 sts plus 2.

Row 1 (RS): Purl.

Row 2 (WS): K1, *[k1, p1, k1] into the next st, p3tog; rep from * to last st, k1.

Row 3: Purl.

Row 4: K1, *p3tog, [k1, p1, k1] into the next st; rep from * to last st, k1.

Rep rows 1–4 for trinity stitch.

Knot Stitch

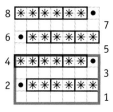

This textured stitch pattern works well for sweaters, jackets, and bags.

Cast on a multiple of 2 sts plus 1.

Rows 1 and 3 (RS): Knit.

Row 2 (WS): K1, *p2tog without slipping sts off the needle, bring yarn to back and knit the same 2 sts together and slide them off the needle; rep from * to end of row.

Row 4: *P2tog without slipping sts off the needle, bring yarn to back and knit the same 2 sts together and slide them off the needle; rep from * to last st, k1.

Rep rows 1–4 for knot stitch.

Pillared Knot Stitch

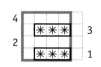

This interesting pattern resembles a rib. It does pull in like a rib, but without a lot of elasticity.

Cast on a multiple of 4 sts plus 1.

Row 1 (RS): K1, *p3tog without slipping sts from the left needle, bring yarn to back and knit the same 3 sts together without slipping sts from the left needle, bring yarn back to the front and purl the 3 sts together (this time slipping the sts off the left needle to complete the knot), k1; rep from * to end of row.

Row 2 (WS): Purl.

Rep rows 1 and 2 for pillared knot stitch.

Star Stitch

In this easy stitch pattern, the little knots resemble stars. This pattern uses the abbreviation *ms*.

ms (make star): P3tog, leaving sts on left needle, then wrap yarn around right needle and purl the same 3 sts together again (this time slipping the sts off the needle to complete the knot).

Cast on a multiple of 4 sts plus 1.

Rows 1 and 3 (RS): Knit.

Row 2 (WS): P1, *ms, p1; rep from * to end of row.

Row 4: P3, ms, *p1, ms; rep from * to last 3 sts, p3.

Rep rows 1–4 for star stitch.

Peppercorn Stitch

This fun nubby stitch gives bags, blankets, and oversized pullovers an eye-catching texture. Making the peppercorn involves reknitting the same stitch three times without increasing; rather, you're adding length to the stitch, not width. Try working it with yarn and needles before questioning it. This pattern begins with a wrong side row.

Cast on a multiple of 4 sts plus 3.

Rows 1 and 3 (WS): Purl.

Row 2 (RS): K3, *k1, [insert left needle into front of st just knit on right needle, and knit it] 3 times, k3; rep from * to end.

NOTE: Inserting the left needle into the front of the st on the right needle and knitting it is similar to what you do when working ssk, but in this case, you're inserting and knitting into one st only. Alternately, you can slip the k1 from the right to left needle each time and reknit it, but it's not as quick.

Row 4: K1, *k1, [insert left needle into front of st just knit on right needle, and knit it] 3 times, k3; rep from *, ending last rep k1 instead of k3.

Rep rows 1–4 for peppercorn stitch.

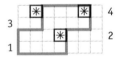

Rosette Stitch

Here is a sweet stitch pattern that looks like rows of roses.

Cast on a multiple of 4 sts plus 3.

Row 1 (RS): P3, *kfbf (3 sts worked in 1 st), p3; rep from * to end.

Row 2 (WS): K3, *p3, k3; rep from * to end.

Row 3: P3, *k3tog, p3; rep from * to end.

Row 4: Knit.

Rep rows 1–4 for rosette stitch.

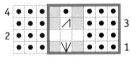

Popcorn Stitch

Popcorns are similar to bobbles, but smaller. Here they're worked on a background of garter stitch. Be sure to leave some slack when knitting three times into the same stitch. This pattern begins with a wrong side row.

Cast on a multiple of 6 sts plus 5.

Rows 1, 2, 3, and 4: Knit.

Row 5 (WS): K5, *[k1, p1, k1, p1] into next st, k5; rep from * to end.

Row 6: K5, *sl 3, k1, pass 3 sl sts one at a time over the last knit st (creating the popcorn), k5; rep from * to end.

Rows 7–10: Knit.

Row 11: K2, *[k1, p1, k1, p1] into next st, k5; rep from *, ending last rep k3 (instead of k5).

Row 12: K2, *sl 3, k1, pass 3 sl sts one at a time over the last knit st, k5; rep from *, ending last rep k2 (instead of k5).

Rep rows 1–12 for popcorn stitch.

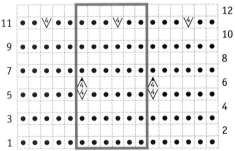

Pompom Stitch

This stitch takes some concentration to work, but the beautiful, high relief pattern is worth the effort. Be sure to work the make 1 (m1) by picking up from front to back the horizontal strand between the last stitch worked and the next stitch on the left needle and knitting it through the front loop. This pattern begins with a wrong side row.

Cast on a multiple of 10 sts plus 2.

Row 1 (WS): K2, *p5, k2, p1, k2; rep from * to end.

Row 2 (RS): P2, *m1, k1, m1, p2, ssk, k1, k2tog, p2; rep from * to end.

Rows 3 and 7: K2, *p3, k2; rep from * to end.

Row 4: P2, *m1, k3, m1, p2, s2kp, p2; rep from * to end.

Row 5: K2, *p1, k2, p5, k2; rep from * to end.

Row 6: P2, *ssk, k1, k2tog, p2, m1, k1, m1, p2; rep from * to end.

Row 8: P2, *s2kp, p2, m1, k3, m1, p2; rep from * to end.

Rep rows 1–8 for pompom stitch.

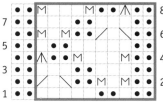

Plait Stitch

Here's a captivating stitch pattern that is worked with two sizes of needles—one the correct size for the yarn, and the other four sizes larger. Cast on to the larger needles.

Cast on an even number of sts.

Row 1 (setup row): Knit using the smaller needle.

Row 2 (WS): Purl using the larger needle. Switch back to the small needle.

NOTE: Now comes the tricky part, where you knit the 2nd st on the left needle and slip it off carefully, then knit the 1st st on the left needle that you passed over. To do so, insert the right needle pwise into the 2nd st on the left needle and lift it over the 1st st, placing it in the 1st st position, and knit it. Then knit the 1st st that you skipped over.

Row 3 (RS): *Knit 2nd st on left needle, knit 1st st on left needle; rep from * to end.

Rep rows 2 and 3 for plait stitch.

Plaited Columns

Here's another way to make your stitches look like braids.

Cast on a multiple of 5 sts.

Row 1 (RS): *K3, sl 1 pwise, k1, yo, psso the k1 and the yo; rep from * to end.

Row 2 (WS): Purl.

Rep rows 1 and 2 for plaited columns.

Vertical Knots

This pattern results in a subtle but rich textured fabric.

Cast on a multiple of 3 sts plus 1.

Row 1 (RS): *K1, sl 1 pwise, k1, psso the k1 and place it on the left needle and knit it; rep from * to last st, k1.

Row 2 (WS): Purl.

Rep rows 1 and 2 for vertical knots.

Chain Stitch

Vertical rows of little links in a chain are easy to make with this stitch pattern.

Cast on a multiple of 7 sts plus 4.

Rows 1 and 3 (RS): P5, *k1, p6; rep from *, ending last rep p5.

Rows 2, 4, and 6 (WS): Work sts as they appear, knitting the knits and purling the purls.

Rows 5 and 7: *P4, k1, p1, k1; rep from * to last 4 sts, p4.

Row 8: Work sts as they appear, knitting the knits and purling the purls.

Rep rows 1–8 for chain stitch.

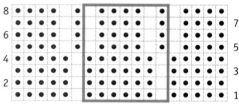

Little Flowers

A delicate pattern like this works well for baby knits and feminine sweaters.

Make flower: K3tog without dropping them from left needle, then re-knit the first st, then knit the 2nd and 3rd sts tog, dropping all off the left needle.

Cast on a multiple of 8 sts plus 1.

Rows 1, 3, 7, and 9 (RS): Knit.

Rows 2, 4, 6, 8, and 10 (WS): Purl.

Row 5: K3, *make flower (k3tog without dropping them from left needle, re-knit the first st, then knit the 2nd and 3rd sts tog, dropping all off the left needle), k5; rep from *, ending last rep k3.

CHAPTER 4

Slipstitch Patterns

Heel Stitch

True to its name, heel stitch is used for sock heels because it's such a durable, solid stitch pattern. But you don't have to use it for heels alone; try it for cushion covers, warm winter sweaters, bags, seat covers—anything that requires a sturdy, dense fabric. This pattern begins with a wrong side row.

Cast on an odd number of sts.

Row 1 (WS): Purl.

Row 2 (RS): K1, *sl 1 wyib, k1; rep from * to end.

Rep rows 1 and 2 for heel stitch.

NOTE: An easy variation of this pattern is knitting on row 1 instead of purling. It has a bumpier texture, with all the strength and warmth of heel stitch.

Simple Slipstitch

This is a very basic slipstitch pattern that works well for cushions or garments that require a dense fabric for a tailored look.

Cast on an odd number of sts.

Row 1 (RS): P1, *sl 1 wyif, p1; rep from * to end.

Row 2 (WS): Knit.

Row 3: Sl 1 wyif, *p1, sl 1 wyif; rep from * to end.

Row 4: Knit.

Rep rows 1–4 for simple slipstitch.

Fluted Slipstitch

This pattern looks similar to ribbing, but it doesn't behave like ribbing. It is reversible, looking the same on both sides.

Cast on a multiple of 4 sts plus 3.

Row 1: K3, *sl 1 wyif, k3; rep from * to end.

Row 2: K1, *sl 1 wyif, k3; rep from * to last 2 sts, sl 1, k1.

Rep rows 1 and 2 for fluted slipstitch.

Bat Stitch

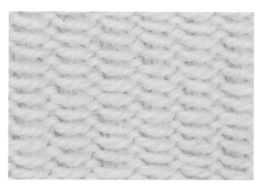

Repeat two simple rows and you have this unique stitch pattern that's appropriate for sweater yokes, tote bags, and much more.

Cast on a multiple of 3 sts plus 1.

Row 1 (RS): Knit.

Row 2 (WS): *K1, sl 2 wyib; rep from * to last st, k1.

Rep rows 1 and 2 for bat stitch.

Pebble Stitch

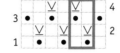

Pebble stitch is similar to double seed stitch, but the slipped stitches lend it a deeper texture. This pattern begins with a wrong side row.

Cast on an odd number of sts.

Row 1 (WS): P1, *k1, p1; rep from * to end.

Row 2 (RS): K1, *sl 1 wyif, k1; rep from * to end.

Row 3: K1, *p1, k1; rep from * to end.

Row 4: K2, *sl 1 wyif, k1; rep from * to last 3 sts, sl 1 pwise wyif, k2.

Rep rows 1–4 for pebble stitch.

Swag Stitch

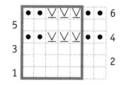

This easy pattern, which has a vintage feel to it, is made by slipping the yarn in front over 3 stitches. This one begins with a wrong side row.

Cast on a multiple of 5 sts plus 2.

Rows 1, 3, and 5 (WS): Purl.

Row 2 (RS): Knit.

Rows 4 and 6: P2, *sl 3 wyif, p2; rep from * to end.

Rep rows 1–6 for swag stitch.

Mock Rib

Another stitch pattern that can be used for just about everything, mock rib is so easy to work that you'll find you've knit several inches without even realizing it.

Cast on a multiple of 2 sts plus 1.

Row 1 (RS): *K1, sl 1 wyif; rep from * to last st, k1.

Row 2 (WS): Purl.

Rep rows 1 and 2 for mock rib.

Double Slipstitch

Double slipstitch is a rugged texture, great for men's sweaters, children's coats, and casual bags.

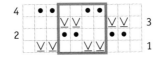

Cast on a multiple of 4 sts plus 2.

Row 1 (RS): K3, *sl 2 wyif, k2; rep from *, ending last rep k1.

Row 2 (WS): P3, *k2, p2; rep from *, ending last rep p1.

Row 3: K1, *sl 2 wyif, k2; rep from *, ending last rep k3.

Row 4: P1, *k2, p2; rep from *, ending last rep p3.

Rep rows 1–4 for double slipstitch.

Linen Stitch

This stitch pattern looks like a flat weave on one side and a rough texture on the other. It lies flat and is wonderful for tailored jackets and coats, as well as throws, cushions, bags, and scarves. Because this fabric pulls itself in so much, you need to use needles that are a few sizes larger than you normally would.

Cast on an even number of sts, using needles that are two or three sizes larger than the size that your yarn calls for.

Row 1 (RS): *K1, sl 1 wyif; rep from * to last 2 sts, k2.

Row 2 (WS): *P1, sl 1 wyib; rep from * to last 2 sts, p2.

Rep rows 1 and 2 for linen stitch.

Double Linen Stitch

This pattern requires large needles so that it isn't too dense to work. Double linen stitch produces a fabric that is so flat and dense that it's really best for things like bags and placemats. Or try using a bulky cotton to make a double linen stitch bath mat.

Cast on a multiple of 4 sts, using needles that are two or three sizes larger than your yarn calls for.

Row 1 (RS): K1, *sl 2 wyif, k2; rep from *, ending last rep k1.

Row 2 (WS): K1, p2, *sl 2 wyib, p2; rep from * to last st, k1.

Rep rows 1 and 2 for double linen stitch.

Slipstitch Tweed

You work the slipped stitches on the right side only of this pattern, which is similar to linen stitch. The purl rows enlarge the weave, and you don't need to use larger needles to work it. It is also known as "half linen stitch."

Cast on an even number of sts.

Row 1 (RS): *K1, sl 1 wyif; rep from * to end.

Row 2 (WS): Purl.

Row 3: *Sl 1 wyif, k1; rep from * to end.

Row 4: Purl.

Rep rows 1–4 for slipstitch tweed.

Herringbone Stitch

Twisting and slipping stitches make this a condensed fabric, good for warm coats and cozy bedspreads; it also makes a nice backdrop to embroidered stitches.

Cast on an even number of sts.

Row 1 (RS): K1, *sl 1-k1-psso but k tbl of sl st before slipping it; rep from * to last st, k1.

Row 2 (WS): *P2tog but keep sts on left needle, purl 1st st again and then drop both sts off needle; rep from * to end.

Rep rows 1 and 2 for herringbone stitch.

⁂⁂ Sl 1-k1-psso but tbl of s1 st before slipping it

⁂⁂ P2tog but keep sts on left needle, purl 1st st again and drop both sts off needle

Diagonal Tweed

The staggered slip stitches create a stair-step motif with this dynamic stitch.

Cast on a multiple of 4 sts plus 2.

Row 1 (RS): *K2, sl 2 wyif; rep from * to last 2 sts, k2.

Rows 2 and 4 (WS): Purl.

Row 3: Sl 1 wyif, *k2, sl 2 wyif; rep from * to last st, k1.

Row 5: Sl 2 wyif, *k2, sl 2 wyif; rep from * to end.

Row 6: Purl.

Row 7: K1, *sl 2 wyif, k2; rep from * to last st, sl 1 wyif.

Row 8: Purl.

Rep rows 1–8 for diagonal tweed.

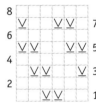

Eyelet Slipstitch

Dropping the yarn overs instead of working them enlarges the eyelets in this pattern, so it's great for lightweight summer knits.

Cast on a multiple of 4 sts.

Row 1 (RS): Knit.

Row 2 (WS): *P4, yo; rep from * to end.

Row 3: *Drop yo (from prev row) off needle, yo, sl 1, k3, psso; rep from * to end.

Row 4: Purl.

Rep rows 1–4 for eyelet slipstitch.

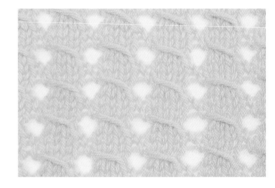

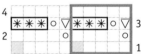 Sl 1, k3, pass slipped st over the 3 knit sts

Slipped 3 x 3 Rib

This beautiful pattern, which is uncomplicated to knit, looks as though it has three layers to it—the 3 x 3 rib on top, the trios of slipped stitches in the middle, and a plain base of knitting on the bottom. In bamboo or stiff linen yarn, this pattern makes an attractive beach bag.

Cast on a multiple of 6 sts plus 5.

Rows 1 and 7 (RS): K4, *p3, k3; rep from * to last st, k1.

Row 2 (WS): K1, p3, *k3, p3; rep from * to last st, k1.

Rows 3 and 5: K4, *sl 3 wyif, k3; rep from * to last st, k1.

Rows 4 and 6: K1, p3, *sl 3 wyib, p3; rep from * to last st, k1.

Row 8: Rep row 2.

Rep rows 1–8 for slipped 3 x 3 rib.

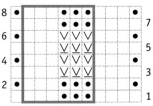

Slipstitch Diamonds

This is a large pattern, best for shawls, throws and oversized sweaters.

Cast on a multiple of 16 sts plus 3.

Row 1 (RS): K4, *sl 2 wyif, k3, sl 1 pwise wyif, k3, sl 2 pwise wyif, k5; rep from *, ending last rep k4.

Row 2 and all even rows (WS): Purl.

Rows 3 and 15: K3, *sl 2 wyif, k3, sl 3 wyif, k3, sl 2 wyif, k2; rep from * ending last rep k3.

Rows 5 and 13: K2, *sl 2 wyif, k3, sl 2 wyif, k1; rep from *, ending last rep k2.

Rows 7 and 11: K1, sl 2 wyif, *[k3, sl 2wyif] twice, k3, sl 3 wyif; rep from *, ending last rep sl 2, k1.

Row 9: K1, *sl 1 wyif, k3, sl 2 wyif, k5, sl 2 wyif, k3; rep from * to last 2 sts, sl 1 wyif, k1.

Row 16: Purl.

Rep rows 1–16 for slipstitch diamonds.

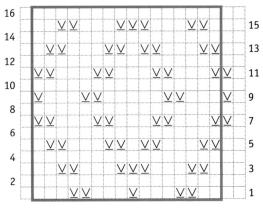

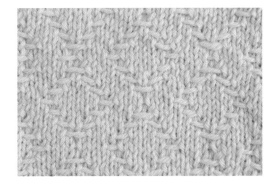

Starlight Stitch

Some people think the slipped stitch motifs that appear in this pattern look like twinkling stars; some think they look like little insects.

Cast on a multiple of 10 sts plus 7.

Rows 1, 3, and 5 (RS): K6, *sl 5 wyif, k5; rep from * to last st, k1.

Rows 2, 4, 8, and 10 (WS): Purl.

Row 6: P8, *using right needle, pull up the 3 sl st strands from underneath and wrap yarn around right needle tip as you would to knit, pulling new loop out from under strands and onto right needle so that the strands are drawn together, purl the next st on the left needle, pass the loop from before over the purled st, p9; rep from *, ending last rep p8.

Rows 7, 9, and 11: K1, *sl 5 wyif, k5; rep from * to last 6 sts, sl 5 wyif, k1.

Row 12: P3, *collect the 3 loose strands as you did in row 6, purl the next st on the left needle and pass loop over the purled st and off the right needle, p9; rep from *, ending last rep p3.

Rep rows 1–12 for starlight stitch.

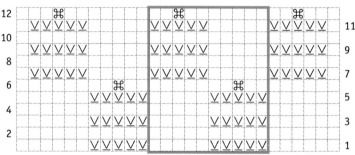

⌘ Using right needle, pull up the 3 sl st strands from underneath and wrap yarn around right needle tip as you would to knit, pulling new loop out from under strands and onto right needle so that the strands are drawn together, purl the next st on the left needle, pass the loop from before over the purled st

Slipstitch Squares

This is a fitting stitch for bed coverlets and similar large items. It wouldn't be the best pattern for baby blankets, however; baby's little fingers will get caught under the slipped stitches.

Cast on a multiple of 12 sts plus 2.

Rows 1, 3, 5, 7, and 9 (RS): K10, sl 3 wyif, *k9, sl 3 wyif; rep from * to last st, k1.

Row 2 and all even rows (WS): Purl.

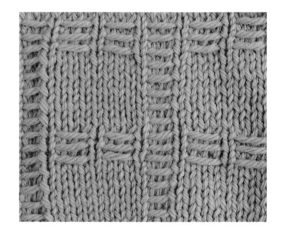

Rows 11, 13, and 15: K2, sl 3 wyif, *k1, sl 3 wyif; rep from * to last st, k1.

Row 16: Purl.

Rep rows 1–16 for slipstitch squares.

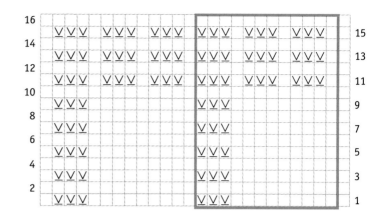

Diamond Weave

Calling this a weave is deceptive; the diamonds look like they are made by weaving the yarns in and out, but they're actually formed by a clever use of slipped stitches. This pattern begins with a wrong side row.

Cast on a multiple of 6 sts plus 3.

Rows 1, 3, 5, and 7 (WS): Purl.

Row 2 (RS): K2, *sl 5 wyif, k1; rep from * to last st, k1.

Row 4: K4, *using right needle, pull up the sl st strand from underneath and knit next st on left needle, pulling new st out from under strand, k5; rep from *, ending last rep k4.

Row 6: K1, sl 3 wyif, *k1, sl 5 wyif; rep from * to last 5 sts, k1, sl 3 wyif, k1.

Row 8: K1, *knit next st from under loose strand (as you did on row 4), k5; rep from *, ending last rep k1.

Rep rows 1–8 for diamond weave.

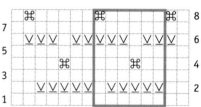

⌘ Using right needle, pull up the sl st strand from underneath and knit next st on left needle, pulling new st out from under strand

Slipstitch Zigzags

It's amazing how some slipstitch patterns create fabrics that look more like weaving than knitting. This pattern is a great example.

Cast on a multiple of 10 sts plus 2.

Row 1 (RS): K2, *sl 3 wyif, k2, sl 3 wyif, k2; rep from * to end.

Row 2 (WS): Sl 1 wyif, *sl 3 wyib, p2; rep from * to last st, sl 1 wyif.

Rows 3 and 9: K1, sl 1 wyif, *k2, sl 3 wyif; rep from * to last 5 sts, k2, sl 2 wyif, st, k1.

Rows 4 and 8: Sl 1 wyif, sl 1 wyib, *p2, sl 3 wyib; rep from * to last 5 sts, p2, sl 2 wyib, sl 1 wyif.

Rows 5 and 7: K1, *sl 3 wyif, k2; rep from * to last st, k1.

Row 6: Sl 1 wyif, p1, *sl 3 wyib, p2; rep from * to last 5 sts, sl 3 wyib, p1, sl 1 wyif.

Row 10: Rep row 2.

Rep rows 1–10 for slipstitch zigzags.

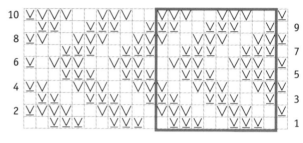

Big Herringbone

Big herringbone looks quite similar to slipstitch zigzags, though not as dense.

Cast on a multiple of 4 sts plus 2.

Rows 1, 5, 9, 15, 19, and 23 (RS): K2, *sl 2 wyif, k2; rep from * to end.

Rows 2, 6, 10, 14, 18, and 22 (WS): P1, *sl 2 wyib, p2; rep from * to last st, p1.

Rows 3, 7, 11, 13, 17, and 21: Sl 2 wyif, *k2, sl 2 wyif; rep from * to end.

Rows 4, 8, 12, 16, 20, and 24: P3, *sl 2 wyib, p2; rep from *, ending last rep p1.

Rep rows 1–24 for big herringbone.

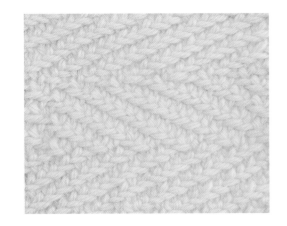

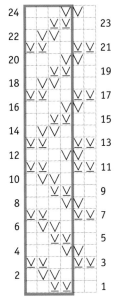

Crisscross

Here's a fun pattern that looks a little like basketweave. It's perfect for outerwear.

Cast on a multiple of 16 sts plus 2.

Row 1 (RS): Knit.

Row 2 (WS): K2, *p6 elongated (purl as usual, but wrap yarn over right needle twice and pull both loops through), k2; rep from * to end.

Row 3: K2, *cross 6 to the right (sl the 6 elongated sts one at a time to the right needle, dropping the extra wrap as you go, then sl the same 6 sts back to the left needle, use the right needle to lift the 4th, 5th and 6th sts on the left needle and place them in front of the first 3 sts on the left needle, then knit the 6 sts in this new order), k2; rep from * to end.

Row 4: P4, k2, *p6 elongated (as in row 2), k2; rep from * to last 4 sts, p4.

Row 5: K6, *cross 6 to the left (sl the 6 elongated sts one at a time to the right needle, dropping the extra wraps as you go; use the left needle to lift the 4th, 5th, and 6th sts on the right needle to the left so that they come before the first 3 sts; sl these 6 sts, maintaining the new order, back to the left needle and knit them), k2; rep from * to last 4 sts, k4.

Rep rows 2–5 for crisscross.

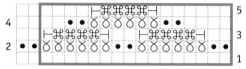

Cross and elongate 6 to the left (sl the 6 elongated sts one at a time to the right needle, dropping the extra wrap as you go; use the left needle to lift the 4th, 5th, and 6th sts on the right needle to the left so that they come before the first 3 sts; sl these 6 sts, maintaining the new order, back to the left needle and knit them)

⊗ K1 elongated on RS; P1 elongated on WS (knit or purl as usual, but wrap yarn over right needle twice and pull both loops through

Slip 5–4–3–2–1

Here's a stitch pattern you rarely see. The number of stitches slipped decreases as you go, which is why the strands form a triangular shape.

Cast on a multiple of 6 sts plus 1.

Row 1 (RS): Knit.

Rows 2 and 8 (WS): Purl.

Rows 3 and 13: K1, *sl 5 wyif, k1; rep from * to end.

Rows 4 and 12: *P2, sl 4 wyib; rep from * to last st, p1.

Rows 5 and 11: K1, *sl 3 wyif, k3; rep from * to end.

Rows 6 and 10: *P4, sl 2 wyib; rep from * to last st, p1.

Rows 7 and 9: K1, *sl 1 wyif, k5; rep from * to end.

Row 14: Purl.

Rep rows 3–14 for slip 5–4–3–2–1.

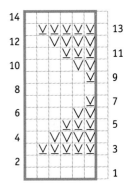

Smocking

There are many forms of knit smocking. Not all employ slipped stitches like this one, which has a lively appeal.

Cast on a multiple of 8 sts plus 7.

Row 1 (RS): K1, *sl 1 wyib, k4, psso the 4 knit sts, k3; rep from *, ending last rep k1 instead of k3.

Row 2 (WS): K1, p1, *k1, m1 (k1 st from underneath horizontal strand between last st worked and next st on the left needle), k1, p5; rep from *, ending last rep p1, k1, instead of p5.

Row 3: K2, *p3, k5; rep from * to last 5 sts, p3, k2.

Row 4: K1, p1, *k3, p5; rep from * to last 5 sts, k3, p1, k1.

Row 5: K2, *p3, sl 1 wyib, k4, psso the 4 knit sts; rep from * to last 5 sts, p3, k2.

Row 6: K1, *p5, k1, m1, k1; rep from * to last 6 sts, p5, k1.

Row 7: K1, *k5, p3; rep from * to last 6 sts, k6.

Row 8: K1, *p5, k3; rep from * to last 6 sts, p5, k1.

Rep rows 1–8 for smocking.

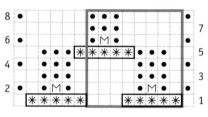

Sl 1 wyib, k4, psso the 4 knit sts

CHAPTER 5

Twist-Stitch Patterns

Twisted Garter Stitch

Knit through the back loop of every other stitch on alternating rows for this easy twist on simple garter stitch.

Cast on an even number of sts.

Row 1 (RS): Knit.

Row 2 (WS): *K1, k1 tbl; rep from * to end.

Rep rows 1 and 2 for twisted garter stitch.

Twisted Stockinette Stitch

Twisting the knit stitches on the right side gives stockinette stitch a striking texture.

Cast on any number of sts.

Row 1 (RS): *K1 tbl; rep from * to end.

Row 2 (WS): Purl.

Rep rows 1 and 2 for twisted stockinette stitch.

Small Zigzags

The "braids" in this pattern are more strikingly jagged, lending the fabric an electric feel. You can use this pattern for just about anything: as an eye-catching framework for Aran cable panels, in cotton for lively looking hand towels, or for a modern women's suit.

Cast on an even number of sts.

Row 1 (RS): *LT; rep from * to end.

Row 2 (WS): *RT; rep from * to end.

Rep rows 1 and 2 for small zigzags.

Small Braids

Easy and simple, small braids is good for both borders and as an allover pattern.

Cast on a multiple of 3 sts plus 1.

Row 1 (RS): *P1, LT; rep from * to last st, p1.

Row 2 (WS): K1, * LT, k1; rep from * to end.

Rep rows 1 and 2 for small braids.

Triple Cord Stitch

This pattern is wonderful for summer shells and cardigans, as well as winter hats.

Cast on a multiple of 9 sts plus 3.

Row 1 (RS): *K3, [LT] 3 times; rep from * to last 3 sts, k3.

Row 2 (WS): Purl.

Rep rows 1 and 2 for triple cord stitch.

Woven Basket Stitch

What a beautiful texture this stitch pattern creates—and it barely looks like knitting.

Cast on an even number of sts.

Row 1 (RS): *LT; rep from * to end.

Row 2 (WS): P1 *RT; rep from * to last st, p1.

Rep rows 1 and 2 for woven basket stitch.

Medium Braid

This braid pattern works well for winter hats; you can increase the number of purl stitches between the braids to allow for decreasing at the crown. This pattern begins with a wrong side row.

Cast on a multiple of 5 sts plus 2.

Rows 1 and 3 (WS): *K2, p3; rep from * to last 2 sts, k2.

Row 2 (RS): P2, *RT, k1, p2; rep from * to end.

Row 4: P2, *k1, LT, p2; rep from * to end.

Rep rows 1–4 for medium braid.

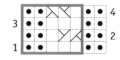

Wasp's Nest Stitch

Here is another easy twist-stitch pattern that works well for throws, pullovers, and cushion covers.

Cast on a multiple of 4 sts.

Row 1 (RS): *RT, LT; rep from * to end.

Rows 2 and 4 (WS): Purl.

Row 3: *LT, RT; rep from * to end.

Rep rows 1–4 for wasp's nest stitch.

Twisted Diagonal Eyelet Stitch

It's surprising that you can create this lovely fabric with a simple four-row repeat. Use this delicate pattern for a women's shell or light summer wrap.

Cast on a multiple of 4 sts plus 3.

Row 1 (RS): P1, RT, *p2, RT; rep from * to end.

Row 2 (WS): K1, *yo, p2tog, k2; rep from * to last 2 sts, yo, p2tog.

Row 3: K1, *p2, RT; rep from * to last 2 sts, p2.

Row 4: K3, *yo, p2tog, k2; rep from * to end.

Rep rows 1–4 for twisted diagonal eyelet stitch.

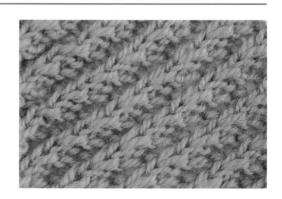

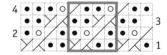

Open Lattice

This pretty stitch pattern is a fitting design for the bodice of a girl's dress, for baby patterns, and for pullovers.

Cast on a multiple of 4 sts plus 2.

Row 1 (RS): P2, *RT, p2; rep from * to end.

Row 2 (WS): K2, *p2, k2; rep from * to end.

Row 3: P1, *k2tog, [yo] twice, ssk; rep from * to last st, p1.

Row 4: P2, *[k1, p1] into the double yo from row 3, p2; rep from * to end.

Row 5: K2, *p2, LT; rep from * to last 4 sts, p2, k2.

Row 6: P2, *k2, p2; rep from * to end.

Row 7: P1, yo, *ssk, k2tog, [yo] twice; rep from * to last 5 sts, ssk, k2tog, yo, p1.

Row 8: K2, *p2, [k1, p1] into double yo from row 7; rep from * to last 4 sts, k2, p2.

Rep rows 1–8 for open lattice.

Wavy Columns

Wavy columns is one of those stitch patterns that makes beautiful borders as well as elegant allover designs. Try it for socks, too.

T3L (twist 3 left—WS): With right needle in front of 1st st on left needle, purl 2nd st, purl 3rd st, then purl 1st st, dropping all 3 original sts from left needle.

T3R (twist 3 right—WS): With right needle behind 1st and 2nd sts on left needle, purl 3rd st, then purl 1st and 2nd st, dropping all 3 original sts from left needle.

Cast on a multiple of 7 sts plus 2.

Rows 1 and 3 (RS): P2, *k5, p2; rep from * to end.

Row 2 (WS): K2, *p1, T3L, p1, k2; rep from * to end.

Row 4: K2, *p1, T3R, p1, k2; rep from * to end.

Rep rows 1–4 for wavy columns.

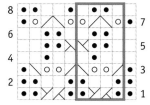

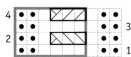

Left Diagonal Twist-Stitch

You can combine this pattern with right diagonal twist stitch that follows to meet in the center of a pullover, throw, bag, or whatever item you're knitting. Or, work the two in opposition to create a dynamic symmetry on cardigan fronts.

Cast on a multiple of 4 sts plus 3.

Row 1 (RS): P1, LT, *p2, LT; rep from * to last 4 sts, p4.

Row 2 (WS): K4, p1, *k3, p1; rep from * to last 2 sts, k2.

Row 3: *P2, LT; rep from * to last 3 sts, p3.

Row 4: K3, *p1, k3; rep from * to end.

Row 5: P3, *LT, p2; rep from * to end.

Row 6: K2, p1, *k3, p1; rep from * to last 4 sts, k4.

Row 7: P4, LT, *p2, LT; rep from * to last st, p1.

Row 8: K1, p1, *k3, p1; rep from * to last 5 sts, k5.

Rep rows 1–8 for left diagonal twist-stitch.

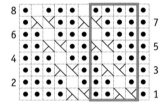

Right Diagonal Twist-Stitch

And here is the mirror-image companion to left diagonal twist-stitch.

Cast on a multiple of 4 sts plus 3.

Row 1 (RS): P4, RT, *p2, RT; rep from * to last st, k1.

Row 2 (WS): K2, p1, *k3, p1; rep from * to last 4 sts, k4.

Row 3: P3, *RT, p2; rep from * to end.

Row 4: K3, *p1, k3; rep from * to end.

Row 5: *P2, RT; rep from * to last 3 sts, p3.

Row 6: K4, p1, *k3, p1; rep from * to last 2 sts, k2.

Row 7: P1, RT, *p2, RT; rep from * to last 4 sts, p4.

Row 8: K5, p1, *k3, p1; rep from * to last st, k1.

Rep rows 1–8 for right diagonal twist-stitch.

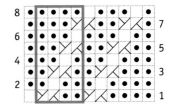

Kernel Stitch

The twisted stitches produce a textural pattern with kernel stitch, making it an excellent addition to Aran sweater designs, casual pullovers, and afghans. This pattern begins with a wrong side row.

Cast on a multiple of 4 sts.

Row 1 (WS): Purl.

Row 2 (RS): K1, p2, *LT, p2; rep from * to last st, k1.

Row 3: K3, *p2, k2; rep from * to last st, k1.

Row 4: K3, *RT, k2; rep from * to last st, k1.

Row 5: Purl.

Row 6: K1, *LT, p2; rep from * to last 3 sts, LT, k1.

Row 7: K1, p2, *k2, p2; rep from * to last st, k1.

Row 8: K1, *RT, k2; rep from * to last 3 sts, RT, k1.

Rep rows 1–8 for kernel stitch.

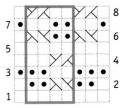

Rosemary

You can use this pattern repeated across the fabric, or as a single repeat panel.

Cast on a multiple of 13 sts.

Row 1 (RS): *K1, RT, k2, RT, k1, LT, k3; rep from * to end.

Row 2 and all even rows (WS): Purl.

Row 3: *K4, RT, k3, LT, k2; rep from * to end.

Row 5: *K3, RT, k1, LT, k2, LT, k1; rep from * to end.

Row 7: *K2, RT, k3, LT, k4; rep from * to end.

Rep rows 1–8 for rosemary.

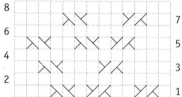

Matchstick Panel (13-Stitch Panel)

The bobbles combined with the crossed twist-stitch diagonals lend this pattern enough depth to frame a bold center cable. This pattern begins with a wrong side row.

Mb (make bobble): Knit into front, back, front, back, and front of next st; without turning work, use left needle to pass 2nd st over the 1st st and off right needle 4 times.

Row 1 and all odd rows (WS): Purl.

Row 2 (RS): K2, LT, k2, RT, k5.

Row 4: K3, LT, RT, k6.

Row 6: K4, LT, k4, mb, k2.

Row 8: K5, LT, k2, RT, k2.

Row 10: K6, LT, RT, k3.

Row 12: K2, mb, k4, RT, k4.

Rep rows 1–12 for matchstick panel.

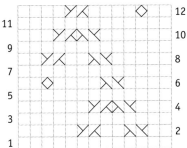

Wishbone Panel (24-Stitch Panel)

The double wishbone motif in this panel boldly rivals cabling. Use it as an element in Aran designs and as a central panel on cardigan fronts and sleeves.

Row 1 (RS): P2, k1 tbl, p2, [LT] twice, p6, [RT] twice, p2, k1 tbl, p2.

Row 2 (WS): K2, p1, k3, p3, k6, p3, k3, p1, k2.

Row 3: P2, k1 tbl, p3, [LT] twice, p4, [RT] twice, p3, k1 tbl, p2.

Row 4: K2, p1, [k4, p3] twice, k4, p1, k2.

Row 5: P2, k1 tbl, p4, [LT] twice, p2, [RT] twice, p4, k1 tbl, p2.

Row 6: K2, p1, k5, p3, k2, p3, k5, p1, k2.

Row 7: P2, k1 tbl, p5, [LT] twice, [RT] twice, p5, k1 tbl, p2.

Row 8: K2, p1, k6, p6, k6, p1, k2.

Row 9: P2, k1 tbl, p6, LT, k2, RT, p6, k1 tbl, p2.

Row 10: K2, p1, k7, p4, k7, p1, k2.

Row 11: P2, k1 tbl, p7, LT, RT, p7, k1 tbl, p2.

Row 12: K2, p1, k2, p3, k3, p2, k3, p3, k2, p1, k2.

Rep rows 1–12 for wishbone panel.

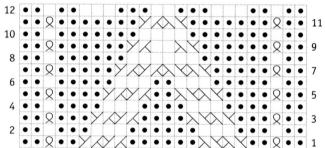

Lattice Stitch

This simple panel can be worked as part of a larger combination of panels and stitch patterns, or by itself centered on a pullover, cushion cover, or cardigan fronts. This pattern begins with a wrong side row.

Cast on a multiple of 6 sts plus 4.

Rows 1 and all odd rows (WS): Purl.

Row 2 (RS): *LT, [RT] twice; rep from * to last 4 sts, LT, RT.

Row 4: K1, LT, *RT, [LT] twice; rep from * to last st, k1.

Row 6: [LT] twice, *k2, [LT] twice; rep from * to end.

Row 8: K1, *[LT] twice, RT; rep from * to last 3 sts, LT, k1.

Row 10: RT, *LT, [RT] twice; rep from * to last 2 sts, LT.

Row 12: K3, *[RT] twice, k2; rep from * to last st, k1.

Rep rows 1–12 for lattice stitch.

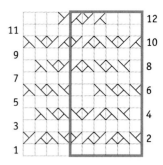

Interlaced Chain Stitch (13-Stitch Panel)

The delicate chain design formed by this stitch pattern has a lovely hand-drawn quality and will never look machine made.

C3Lp: Sl 2 sts to cn and hold at front, k1 tbl from left needle, sl center st from cn back to left needle and purl it, k1 tbl fron cn.

C3Rp: Sl 2 to cn and hold at back, k1 tbl from left needle, sl center st from cn back to left needle and purl it, k1 tbl from cn.

Rows 1, 17, and 19 (RS): P2, k1 tbl, p1, k1 tbl, p3, k1 tbl, p1, k1 tbl, p2.

Rows 2, 16, and 18 (WS): K2, p1 tbl, k1, p1 tbl, k3, p1 tbl, k1, p1 tbl, k2.

Row 3: P2, C3Lp, p3, C3Lp, p2.

Row 4: K1, [LT, k1, RT, k1] twice.

Row 5: P1, k1 tbl, p3, C3Rp, p3, k1 tbl, p1.

Rows 6, 8, 10, and 12: K1, [p1 tbl, k3, p1 tbl, k1] twice.

Rows 7, 9, and 11: P1, [k1 tbl, p3, k1 tbl, p1] twice.

Row 13: P1, k1 tbl, p3, C3Lp, p3, k1 tbl, p1.

Row 14: K1, [LT, k1, RT, k1] twice.

Row 15: P2, C3Rp, p3, C3Rp, p2.

Row 20: K2, p1 tbl, k1, p1 tbl, k3, p1 tbl, k1, p1 tbl, k2.

Rep rows 1–20 for interlaced chain stitch.

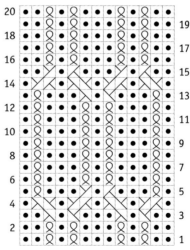

 C3Lp

 C3Rp

Mock Ribbed Cables

This beautiful allover pattern is perfect for women's sweaters, bedspreads, cushion covers, and socks.

LTp: Skip 1st st, purl 2nd st tbl but leave on needle, knit skipped st, then drop both original sts from left needle.

RTp: Skip 1st st, knit 2nd st but leave on needle, purl skipped st, then drop both original sts from left needle.

C3R: Sl next 2 sts to cn and hold at back, k1 tbl, k tbl the 2 sts on cn.

Cast on a multiple of 12 sts plus 1.

Row 1 (RS): P1, *[k1 tbl, p1] 3 times, LTp, k1 tbl, RTp, p1; rep from * to end.

Row 2 and all even rows (WS): Work each st as it appears, purling tbl the sts that were knit tbl on the prev row.

Row 3: P1, *k1 tbl, [p1, k1 tbl] twice, p2, C3R, p2; rep from * to end.

Row 5: P1, *[k1 tbl, p1] 3 times, RTp, k1 tbl, LTp, p1; rep from * to end.

Rows 7 and 15: P1, *k1 tbl, p1; rep from * to end.

Row 9: P1, *LTp, k1 tbl, RTp, p1, [k1 tbl, p1] 3 times; rep from * to end.

Row 11: *P2, C3R, p2, k1 tbl, [p1, k1 tbl] twice; rep from * to last st, p1.

Row 13: P1, *RTp, k1 tbl, LTp, [p1, k1 tbl] 3 times, p1; rep from * to end.

Row 15: Rep row 2.

Rep rows 1–16 for mock ribbed cables.

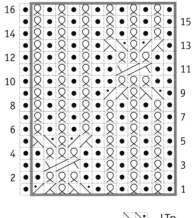

	LTp
	RTp
	C3R

Half-Filled Diamond Cable

You can use this as a repeating pattern, but it also works perfectly as a center panel.

RTp: Skip 1st st, knit 2nd st but leave on needle, purl skipped st, then drop both original sts from left needle.

Cast on a multiple of 13 sts.

Row 1 (RS): P6, *LT, p11; rep from *, ending last rep p5.

Row 2 and all even (WS) rows: Work sts as they appear.

Row 3: P5, *RTp, LT, p9; rep from *, ending last rep p4.

Row 5: P4, *[RTp] twice, LT, p7; rep from *, ending last rep p3.

Row 7: P3, *[RTp] 3 times, LT, p5; rep from *, ending last rep p2.

Row 9: P2, *[RTp] 3 times, p2, k1, p4; rep from *, ending last rep p2.

Row 11: P3, *[RTp] twice, p3, k1, p5; rep from *, ending last rep p2.

Row 13: P4, *RTp, p3, RTp, p6; rep from *, ending last rep p2.

Row 15: P8, *RTp, p11; rep from *, ending last rep p3.

Row 17: P7, *RTp, p11; rep from *, ending last rep p4.

Row 19: P6, *RT, p11; rep from *, ending last rep p5.

Rep rows 1–20 for half-filled diamond cable.

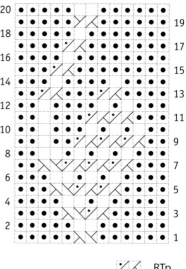

RTp

Twist-Stitch Leaf

It's easy to work this lovely leaf-motif pattern, which is fitting for baby sweaters, women's skirts, socks, and more.

Cast on a multiple of 14 sts.

Rows 1 and 5 (RS): *K2, RT, LT, k8; rep from * to end.

Row 2 and all even rows (WS): Purl.

Row 3: *K1, RT, k2, LT, k7; rep from * to end.

Row 7: *K3, RT, k9; rep from * to end.

Row 9: Knit.

Rows 11 and 15: *K8, RT, LT, k2; rep from * to end.

Row 13: *K7, RT, k2, LT, k1; rep from * to end.

Row 17: *K9, RT, k3; rep from * to end.

Row 19: Knit.

Rep rows 1–20 for twist-stitch leaf pattern.

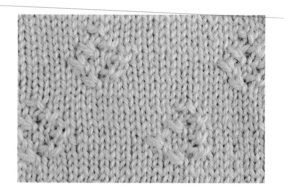

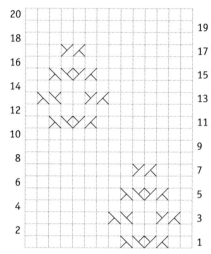

Alternating Zigzags

The movement of the zigzags in this pattern is enhanced by alternating stockinette stitch and reverse stockinette stitch within the vertical zigzags.

Cast on a multiple of 14 sts.

Row 1 (RS): *P5, RT, k4, RT, p1; rep from * to end.

Row 2 and all even rows (WS): Work the sts as they appear.

Row 3: *P4, RT, k4, RT, p2; rep from * to end.

Row 5: *P3, RT, k4, RT, p3; rep from * to end.

Row 7: *P2, RT, k4, RT, p4; rep from * to end.

Row 9: *P1, RT, k4, RT, p5; rep from * to end.

Row 11: *P1, LT, k4, LT, p5; rep from * to end.

Row 13: *P2, LT, k4, LT, p4; rep from * to end.

Row 15: *P3, LT, k4, LT, p3; rep from * to end.

Row 17: *P4, LT, k4, LT, p2; rep from * to end.

Row 19: *P5, LT, k4, LT, p1; rep from * to end.

Rep rows 1–20 for alternating zigzags.

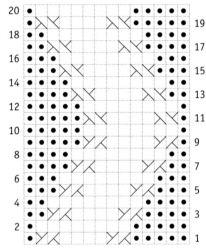

Peanuts

This playful pattern works beautifully on bags and cushion covers. It begins with a wrong side row.

Cast on a multiple of 12 sts plus 4.

Rows 1, 7, and 13 (WS): *K1, RT, k10; rep from * to last 3 sts, RT, k1.

Rows 2 and 8 (RS): RT, LT, *p8, RT, LT; rep from * to end.

Rows 3, 5, 9, and 11: *P4, k8; rep from * to last 4 sts, p4.

Rows 4 and 10: K4, *p8, k4; rep from * to end.

Rows 6 and 12: LT, RT, *p8, LT, RT; rep from * to end.

Rows 14 and 28: Purl.

Rows 15, 21, and 27: *K7, RT, k3; rep from * to last 4 sts, k4.

Rows 16 and 22: P4, *p2, RT, LT, p6; rep from * to end.

Rows 17, 19, 23, and 25: *K6, p4, k2; rep from * to last 4 sts, k4.

Rows 18 and 24: P4, *p2, k4, p6; rep from * to end.

Rows 20 and 26: P4, *p2, LT, RT, p6; rep from * to end.

Rep rows 1–28 for peanuts.

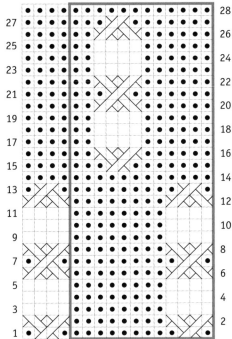

Broken Lattice

This pattern is similar to lattice. It diverges in at alternating points with interruptions in the lines of the lattice, which results in a pattern that is more complex to the eye. Use it for women's coats, skirts, cushion covers, and washcloths.

Cast on a multiple of 2 sts.

Rows 1, 3, 5, and 7 (WS): Purl.

Row 2 (RS): *LT, k2, LT, RT; rep from * to end.

Row 4: K1, *LT, k2, RT, k2; rep from *, ending last rep k1.

Row 6: *RT, LT, RT, k2; rep from * to end.

Row 8: K3, *LT, k2, RT, k2; rep from * to last 5 sts, LT, k3.

Rep rows 1–8 for broken lattice.

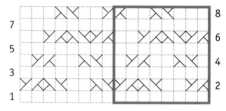

CHAPTER 6

Cable Patterns

4-Stitch Right Cable (C4B)

This basic cable is worked on six stitches and twists to the right. This version separates the cables with two purl stitches, but you can alter that to suit your design.

C4B: Sl next 2 sts to cn and hold at back of work, k2 from left needle, then k2 from cn.

Cast on a multiple of 6 sts plus 2.

Row 1 (RS): P2, *k4, p2; rep from * to end.

Row 2 (WS): K2, *p4, k2; rep from * to end.

Row 3 (cable row): P2, *C4B , p2; rep from * to end.

Row 4: Rep row 2.

Rep rows 1–4 for 4-stitch right cable.

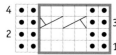

4-Stitch Left Cable (C4F)

This is the mirror image to the right cable, so it twists to the left.

C4F: Sl next 2 sts to cn and hold at front of work, k2 from left needle, k2 from cn.

Cast on a multiple of 6 sts plus 2.

Row 1 (RS): P2, *k4, p2; rep from * to end.

Row 2 (WS): K2, *p4, k2; rep from * to end.

Row 3 (cable row): P2, *C4F, p2; rep from * to end.

Row 4: Rep row 2.

Rep rows 1–4 for 4-stitch left cable.

TIP

Elongating the Cables

You can elongate the cables on this and the following pages by adding plain rows between the cable rows. For instance, repeat rows 1 and 2 once more to make a 6-row version, or twice more for an 8-row version. Or alternate turning the cable every 4th row and every 8th row to add visual interest to this simple cable pattern.

6-Stitch Right Cable (C6B)

This basic cable is worked on six stitches and twists to the right. This version separates the cables with two purl stitches, but you can alter that to suit your design.

C6B: Sl next 3 sts to cn and hold at back of work, k3 from left needle, k3 from cn.

Cast on a multiple of 8 sts plus 2.

Row 1 (RS): P2, *k6, p2; rep from * to end.

Row 2 (WS): K2, *p6, k2; rep from * to end.

Row 3 (cable row): P2, *C6B, p2; rep from * to end.

Row 4: Rep row 2.

Rep rows 1–4 for 6-stitch right cable.

6-Stitch Left Cable (C6F)

This is the mirror image to the right cable, so it twists to the left.

C6F: Sl next 3 sts to cn and hold at front of work, k3 from left needle, then k3 from cn.

Cast on a multiple of 8 sts plus 2.

Row 1 (RS): P2, *k6, p2; rep from * to end.

Row 2 (WS): K2, *p6, k2; rep from * to end.

Row 3 (cable row): P2, *C6F, p2; rep from * to end.

Row 4: Rep row 2.

Rep rows 1–4 for 6-stitch left cable.

8-Stitch Right Cable (C8B)

This basic cable is worked on eight stitches and twists to the right. This version separates the cables with two purl stitches, but you can alter that to suit your design.

C8B: Sl next 4 sts to cn and hold at back of work, k4 from left needle, k4 from cn.

Cast on a multiple of 10 sts plus 2.

Row 1 (RS): P2, *k8, p2; rep from * to end.

Row 2 (WS): K2, *p8, k2; rep from * to end.

Row 3 (cable row): P2, *C8B, p2; rep from * to end.

Row 4: Rep row 2.

Rep rows 1–4 for 8-stitch right cable.

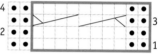

8-Stitch Left Cable (C8F)

This is the mirror image to the right cable, so it twists to the left.

C8F: Sl next 4 sts to cn and hold at front of work, k4 from left needle, k4 from cn.

Cast on a multiple of 10 sts plus 2.

Row 1 (RS): P2, *k8, p2; rep from * to end.

Row 2 (WS): K2, *p8, k2; rep from * to end.

Row 3 (cable row): P2, *C8F, p2; rep from * to end.

Row 4: Rep row 2.

Rep rows 1–4 for 8-stitch left cable.

10-Stitch Right Cable (C10B)

This basic cable is worked on ten stitches and twists to the right. This version separates the cables with two purl stitches, but you can alter that to suit your design.

C10B: Sl next 5 sts to cn and hold at back of work, k5 from left needle, k5 from cn.

Cast on a multiple of 12 sts plus 2.

Row 1 (RS): P2, *k10, p2; rep from * to end.

Row 2 (WS): K2, *p10, k2; rep from * to end.

Row 3 (cable row): P2, *C10B, p2; rep from * to end.

Row 4: Rep row 2.

Rep rows 1–4 for 10-stitch right cable.

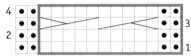

10-Stitch Left Cable (C10F)

This is the mirror image to the right cable, so it twists to the left.

C10F: Sl next 5 sts to cn and hold at front of work, k5 from left needle, k5 from cn.

Cast on a multiple of 12 sts plus 2.

Row 1 (RS): P2, *k10, p2; rep from * to end.

Row 2 (WS): K2, *p10, k2; rep from * to end.

Row 3 (cable row): P2, *C10F, p2; rep from * to end.

Row 4: Rep row 2.

Rep rows 1–4 for 10-stitch left cable.

Braided Cable (12-Stitch Panel)

This cable is easier to make than it looks.

C4B: Sl next 2 sts to cn and hold at back of work, k2 from left needle, k2 from cn.

C4F: Sl next 2 sts to cn and hold at front of work, k2 from left needle, k2 from cn.

Row 1 (RS—cable row): P2, (C4B) twice, p2.

Row 2 (WS): K2, p8, k2.

Row 3 (cable row): P2, k2, C4F, k2, p2.

Row 4: Rep row 2.

Rep rows 1–4 for braided cable.

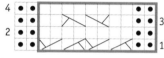

Woven Cable Stitch

This pattern looks like real basketweave.

C4F: Sl next 2 sts to cn and hold at front of work, k2 from left needle, k2 from cn.

C4B: Sl next 2 sts to cn and hold at back of work, k2 from left needle, k2 from cn.

Cast on a multiple of 4 sts.

Row 1 (RS—cable row): *C4F; rep from * to end.

Row 2 (WS): Purl.

Row 3 (cable row): K2, *C4B; rep from * to last 2 sts, k2.

Row 4: Rep row 2.

Rep rows 1–4 for woven cable stitch.

Horn Cable (16-Stitch Panel)

Here's a cable that looks important enough to take center stage but is also simple enough to frame a larger cable.

C4B: Sl next 2 sts to cn and hold at back of work, k2 from left needle, k2 from cn.

C4F: Sl next 2 sts to cn and hold at front of work, k2 from left needle, k2 from cn.

Row 1 (RS—cable row): K4, C4B, C4F, k4.

Rows 2 and 4 (WS): Purl.

Row 3 (cable row): K2, C4B, k4, C4F, k2.

Row 5 (cable row): C4B, k8, C4F.

Row 6: Rep row 2.

Rep rows 1–6 for horn cable.

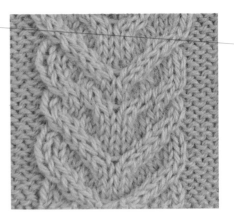

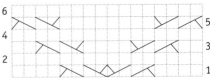

Big Cable (16-Stitch Panel)

This cable twists to the right, but you can make its mirror image—a big cable that twists to the left—by holding the stitches on the cable needle in the front instead of the back of the work on row 5. The cable is centered between two sets of two purl stitches, but you can modify this for your own design.

C12B: Sl next 6 sts to cn and hold at back, k6 sts from left needle, k6 from cn.

Rows 1, 3, and 7 (RS): P2, k12, p2.

Rows 2, 4, and 6, (WS): K2, p12, k2.

Row 5 (cable row): P2, C12B, p2.

Row 8: Rep row 2.

Rep rows 1–8 for big cable.

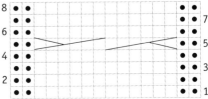

Wave Cable (10-Stitch Panel)

Performing both the front cross and back cross in the same cable makes this playful panel.

C6B: Sl next 3 sts to cn and hold at back of work, k3 from left needle, k3 from cn.

C6F: Sl next 3 sts to cn and hold at front of work, k3 from left needle, k3 from cn.

Rows 1, 5, 7, and 11 (RS): P2, k6, p2.

Rows 2, 4, 6, 8, and 10 (WS): K2, p6, k2.

Row 3 (cable row): P2, C6B, p2.

Row 9 (cable row): P2, C6F, p2.

Row 12: Rep row 2.

Rep rows 1–12 for wave cable.

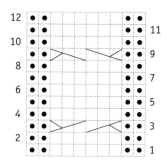

Double Cable (12-Stitch Panel)

You can make this cable so that it looks like it's pointing upward (shown on the left) or downward (shown on the right). Here's how to make a downward-pointing cable.

C4F: Sl next 2 sts to cn and hold at front of work, k2 from left needle, k2 from cn.

C4B: Sl next 2 sts to cn and hold at back of work, k2 from left needle, k2 from cn.

Rows 1, 5, and 7 (RS): P2, k8, p2.

Rows 2, 4, and 6 (WS): K2, p8, k2.

Row 3 (cable row): P2, C4F, C4B, p2.

Row 8: Rep row 2.

Rep rows 1–8 for double cable.

NOTE: To make the cable point upward, work all rows the same way, but work row 3 as p2, C4B, C4F, p2.

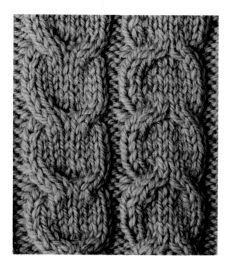

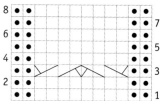

Wishbone and Seed Stitch Cable (12-Stitch Panel)

This delicate cable looks complicated but is easy to do.

4-st RMC (4-stitch right moss stitch cable): Sl next 3 sts to cn and hold at back, k1 from left needle, then p1, k1, p1 from cn.

4-st LMC (4-stitch left moss stitch cable): Sl next st to cn and hold at front, k1, p1, k1 from left needle, then k1 from cn.

Row 1 (RS—cable row): P2, 4-st RMC; 4-st LMC; p2.

Rows 2, 4, and 6 (WS): K2, [p1, k1] 3 times, p2, k2.

Rows 3 and 5: P2, [k1, p1] 3 times, k2, p2.

Row 7: P2, k1, p1, k3, p1, k2, p2.

Row 8: K2, p1, k1, p3, k1, p2, k2.

Rep rows 1–8 for wishbone and seed stitch cable.

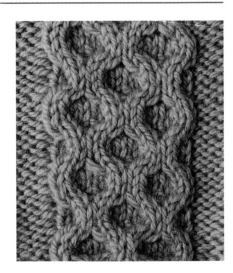

Honeycomb Cable (20-Stitch Panel)

You can widen this interesting cable by adding multiples of 8 stitches.

C4B: Sl next 2 sts to cn and hold at back of work, k2 from left needle, k2 from cn.

C4F: Sl next 2 sts to cn and hold at front of work, k2 from left needle, k2 from cn.

Row 1 (RS—cable row): P2, [C4B, C4F] twice, p2.

Rows 2, 4, and 6 (WS): K2, p16, k2.

Rows 3 and 7: P2, k16, p2.

Row 5 (cable row): P2, [C4F, C4B] twice, p2.

Row 8: Rep row 2.

Rep rows 1–8 for honeycomb cable.

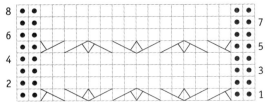

Ladders and Cables

The openwork in this pattern makes it fitting for summer sweaters and wraps. This pattern begins with a wrong side row.

C6B: Sl next 3 sts to cn and hold at back of work, k3 from left needle, k3 from cn.

C6F: Sl next 3 sts to cn and hold at front of work, k3 from left needle, k3 from cn.

Cast on a multiple of 14 sts plus 1.

Row 1 and all odd rows (WS): K1, *p2tog, yo, p11, k1; rep from * to end.

Row 2 (RS—cable row): K1, *ssk, yo, C6B, k6; rep from * to end.

Row 4: K1, *ssk, yo, k12; rep from * to end.

Row 6 (cable row): K1, *ssk, yo, k3, C6F, k3; rep from * to end.

Row 8: Rep row 4.

Rep rows 1–8 for ladders and cables.

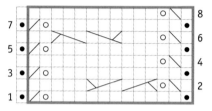

Knotted Cable (10-Stitch Panel)

This cable involves moving the cable needle from front to back and working the held stitches in stages.

Rows 1, 5, 7, and 9 (RS): P2, k2, p2, k2, p2.

Rows 2, 4, 6, and 8 (WS): P4, k2, p4.

Row 3 (cable row): P2, sl next 4 sts to cn and hold at front, knit next 2 sts from left needle; then sl 2 sts from cn back to left needle. Bring cn (with rem 2 sts on it) to back, p2 (sts that were returned to left needle); k2 sts from the cn, p2.

Row 10: Rep row 2.

Rep rows 1–10 for knotted cable.

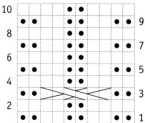

Tulip Cables

This is a captivating allover pattern that can also be used for hems and cuffs.

C4B: Sl next 2 sts to cn and hold at back of work, k2 from left needle, k2 from cn.

C4F: Sl next 2 sts to cn and hold at front of work, k2 from left needle, k2 from cn.

Cast on a multiple of 8 sts.

Rows 1, 5, 7, and 9 (RS): P2, *K4, P4; rep from * to last 6 sts, k4, p2.

Row 2 and all even rows (WS): Purl.

Row 3 (cable row): *C4B, C4F; rep from * to end.

Row 10: Purl.

Rep rows 1–10 for tulip cables.

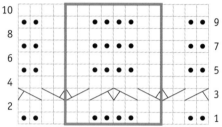

Bobble Cable (13-Stitch Panel)

Here's a cable that's easy and fun to work. If you omit the bobbles, you have a nice open cable.

3-st RPC: Sl next st to cn and hold at back, k2 from left needle, p1 from cn.

3-st LPC: Sl next 2 sts to cn and hold at front, p1 from left needle, k2 from cn.

Mb (make bobble): Knit into front, back, front, back, and front of next st; without turning work, use left needle to pass 2nd, 3rd, 4th, and 5th st over 1st st and off right needle one at a time.

Row 1 (RS—cable row): P3, 3-st RPC, p1, 3-st LPC, p3.

Rows 2 and 8 (WS): K3, p2, k3, p2, k3.

Row 3 (cable row): P2, 3-st RPC, p3, 3-st LPC, p2.

Rows 4 and 6: K2, p2, k5, p2, k2.

Row 5 (bobble row): P2, k2, p2, mb, p2, k2, p2.

Row 7 (cable row): P2, 3-st LPC, p3, 3-st RPC, p2.

Row 9 (cable row): P3, 3-st LPC, p1, 3-st RPC, p3.

Row 10: K4, p5, k4.

Row 11 (cable row): P4, sl next 3 sts to cn and hold at back, knit next 2 sts from left needle, then p1, k2 from cn, p4.

Row 12: Rep row 10.

Rep rows 1–12 for bobble cable.

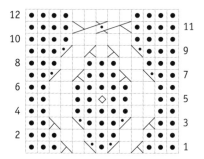

Landscape Cables

These cables form a deeply textured fabric that is mesmerizing to the eye. It makes fabulous cushion covers, throws, and oversized jackets and pullovers.

C10F: Sl next 5 sts to cn and hold at front of work, k5 from left needle, k5 from cn.

C10B: Sl next 5 sts to cn and hold at back of work, k5 from left needle, k5 from cn.

Cast on a multiple of 15 sts plus 2.

Rows 1, 5, 7, and 11 (RS): Knit.

Rows 2, 4, 6, 8, and 10 (WS): Purl.

Row 3 (cable row): K1, C10F, *k5, C10F; rep from * to last 6 sts, k6.

Row 9 (cable row): K6, C10B, *k5, C10B; rep from * to last st, k1.

Row 12: Purl.

Rep rows 1–12 for landscape cables.

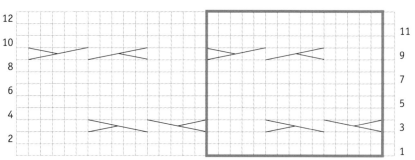

Trellis Cable Stitch

This allover pattern is excellent for items such as pillow covers, throws, women's suits, and girls' dresses.

Cast on a multiple of 6 sts.

T3B: Sl 2 sts onto cn and hold at back of work, k1 from left needle, p2 from cn.

T3F: Sl 1 st onto cn and hold at front of work, p2 from left needle, k1 from cn.

Rows 1, 3, and 13 (RS): P2, *k2, p4; rep from * to last 4 sts, k2, p2.

Row 2 and all even rows (WS): Work sts as they appear.

Row 5 (cable row): *T3B, T3F; rep from * to end.

Rows 7 and 9: K1, *p4, k2; rep from * to last 5 sts, p4, k1.

Row 11 (cable row): *T3F, T3B; rep from * to end.

Row 14: Rep row 2.

Rep rows 1–14 for trellis cable stitch.

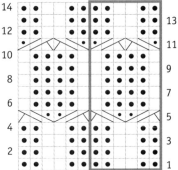

Ribbed Cable (15-Stitch Panel)

This interesting cable is worked in k1, p1 ribbing.

Rows 1, 5, 7, 9, 11, and 13 (RS): P2, k1, [p1, k1] 5 times, p2.

Rows 2, 4, 6, 8, 10, and 12 (WS): K2, p1 tbl, [k1, p1 tbl] 5 times, k2.

Row 3 (cable row): P2, sl next 6 sts to cn and hold at back, k1, [p1, k1] twice from left needle, then [p1, k1] 3 times from cn; p2.

Row 14: Rep row 2.

Rep rows 1–14 for ribbed cable.

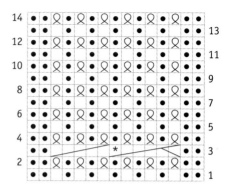

Nautical Cable (24-Stitch Panel)

Here's a traditional cable that is perfect for fishermen's knits.

C6F: Sl next 3 sts to cn and hold at front of work, k3 from left needle, k3 from cn.

C6B: Sl next 3 sts to cn and hold at back of work, k3 from left needle, k3 from cn.

T5F: Sl the next 3 sts to cn and hold at front, purl the next 2 sts on left needle, k3 from cn.

T5B: Sl the next 2 sts to cn and hold at back, k3 from left needle, p2 from cn.

Rows 1 and 5 (RS): P2, k3, p4, k6, p4, k3, p2.

Row 2 and all even rows (WS): Work sts as they appear.

Row 3 (cable row): P2, k3, p4, C6F, p4, k3, p2.

Row 7 (cable row): P2, T5F, p2, k6, p2, T5B, p2.

Row 9 (cable row): P4, T5F, C6F, T5B, p4.

Row 11 (cable row): P6, [C6B] twice, p6.

Row 13 (cable row): P4, T5B, C6F, T5F, p4.

Row 15 (cable row): P2, T5B, p2, k6, p2, T5F, p2.

Row 16: Rep row 2.

Rep rows 1–16 for nautical cable.

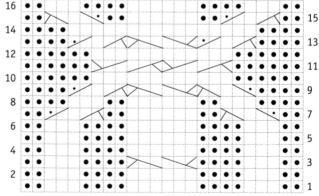

Twist-Stitch Medallion Cable (19-Stitch Panel)

The addition of twisted stitches refines this striking cable. This pattern begins with a wrong side row.

C6F-tbl: Sl next 3 sts to dpn and hold at front, k3 tbl from left needle, k3 tbl from cn.

C6B-tbl: Sl next 3 sts to dpn and hold at back, k3 tbl from left needle, k3 tbl from cn.

Rows 1, 3, 5, 7, 9, 11, 13, and 15 (WS): K2, p15 tbl, k2.

Row 2 (RS—cable row): P2, C6F-tbl, k3 tbl, C6B-tbl, p2.

Rows 4, 6, 10, 12, and 14: P2, k15 tbl, p2.

Row 8 (cable row): P2, C6B-tbl, k3 tbl, C6F-tbl, p2.

Row 16: Rep row 4.

Rep rows 1–16 for twist-stitch medallion cable.

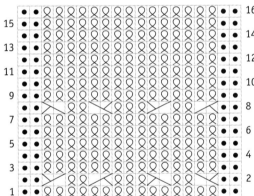

Rectangular Cable

Have fun with this geometric twist on a classic cable. Here it is centered between two sets of two purl stitches, but you can modify it to suit your design.

C8F: Sl next 4 sts to cn and hold at front of work, k4 from left needle, k4 from cn.

Cast on a multiple of 10 sts plus 2.

Rows 1, 5, 7, 11, and 15 (RS): P2, *k8, p2; rep from * to end.

Rows 2, 4, 6, and 14 (WS): K2, *p8, k2; rep from * to end.

Row 3 (cable row): P2, *C8F, p2; rep from * to end.

Rows 8, 10, and 12: K2, *p2, k4, p2, k2; rep from * to end.

Rows 9, 11, and 13: P2, *k2, p4, k2, p2; rep from * to end.

Row 16: Rep row 2.

Rep rows 1–16 for rectangular cable.

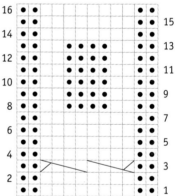

Openwork Sausage Cables

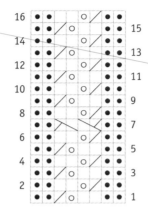

You can work this unique and pretty cable as a single panel of 8 stitches, with the 4-stitch cable set between two sets of two purl stitches.

C4F: Sl next 2 sts to cn and hold at front of work, k2 from left needle, k2 from cn.

Cast on a multiple of 6 sts plus 2.

Rows 1, 3, 5, 9, 11, 13, and 15 (RS): P2, *k2, yo, k2tog, p2; rep from * to end.

Row 2 and all even rows (WS): K2, *p2, yo, p2tog, k2; rep from * to end.

Row 7 (cable row): P2, *C4F, p2; rep from * to end.

Row 16: Rep row 2.

Rep rows 1–16 for openwork sausage cables.

Banjo Cable (12-Stitch Panel)

Banjo cable is a delightful addition to cabled pullovers, cardigans, and afghans. This pattern begins with a wrong side row.

4-st RMC (4-stitch right moss stitch cable): Sl next 3 sts to cn and hold at back, k1 from left needle, then p1, k1, p1 from cn.

4-st LMC (4-stitch left moss stitch cable): Sl next st to cn and hold at front, k1, p1, k1 from left needle, then k1 from cn.

4-st LPT (4-stitch left purl twist): Sl next st to cn and hold at front, p2, k1 from left needle, then k1 from cn.

4-st RPT (4-stitch right purl twist): Sl next 3 sts to cn and hold at back, k1 from left needle, then k1, p2 from cn.

Rows 1, 13, and 15 (WS): K4, p4, k4.

Rows 2 and 14 (RS): P4, k4, p4.

Row 3: K4, p1, sl 2 sts wyif, p1, k4.

Row 4 (cable row): P2, 4-st RMC, 4-st LMC, p2.

Rows 5, 7, and 9: K2, [p1, k1] 3 times, p2, k2.

Rows 6, 8, and 10: P2, [k1, p1] 3 times, k2, p2.

Row 11: K2, sl 1 wyif, [k1, p1] 3 times, sl 1 wyif, k2.

Row 12 (cable row): P2, 4-st LPT, 4-st RPT, p2.

Row 16: Rep row 2.

Rep rows 1–16 for banjo cable.

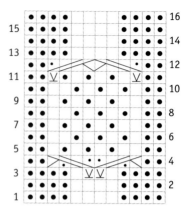

Cabled Checkerboard

This is a wonderful allover pattern that is suitable for just about anything—bags, blankets, suits, and sweaters.

C4B: Sl next 2 sts to cn and hold at back of work, k2 from left needle, k2 from cn.

Cast on a multiple of 10 sts plus 6.

Row 1 (RS): P1, *k4, p6; rep from * to last 5 sts, k4, p1.

Row 2 and all even rows (WS): Work sts as they appear.

Rows 3, 7, 11, and 15: Work sts as they appear.

Row 5 (cable row): P1, *C4B, p6; rep from * to last 5 sts, C4B, p1.

Row 9: P6, *k4, p6; rep from * to end.

Row 13 (cable row): P6, *C4B, p6; rep from * to end.

Row 16: Rep row 2.

Rep rows 1–16 for cabled checkerboard.

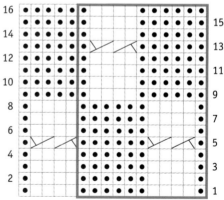

Tuning Fork Cable
(16-Stitch Panel)

Here's an interesting cable that deserves to be the center of attention. Note how the lines of garter stitch intersecting the cable mimic the vibration of the tuning fork.

T6R: Sl next 4 sts to cn and hold at back, k2 from left needle, then p2, k2 from cn.

T6L: Sl next 2 sts to cn and hold at front, k2, p2 from left needle, then k2 from cn.

Rows 1, 3, 5, 9, and 11 (RS): P2, k2, p2, k4, p2, k2, p2.

Rows 2, 4, 6, 8, and 10 (WS): K2, p2, k2, p4, k2, p2, k2.

Row 7 (cable row): P2, sl next 4 sts to cn and hold at back, k2 from left needle, then p2, k2 from cn, sl next 2 sts to cn and hold at front, k2, p2 from left needle, then k2 from cn, p2.

Rows 12–16: Knit.

Rep rows 1–16 for tuning fork cable.

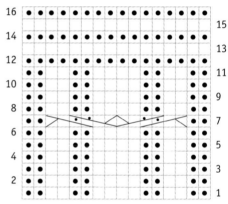

Diamonds and Circles Cable (26-Stitch Panel)

Strategically placed increases and decreases help to achieve this cable's unusual contortions. Be sure to keep track of your stitch count as you go, as it will vary.

C4B: Sl next 2 sts to cn and hold at back of work, k2 from left needle, k2 from cn.

C4F: Sl next 2 sts to cn and hold at front of work, k2 from left needle, k2 from cn.

T4B: Sl next 2 sts onto cn and hold at back, k2 from left needle, p2 from cn.

T4F: Sl next 2 sts to cn and hold at front, p2 from left needle, k2 from cn.

Row 1 (RS): P11, k4, p11.

Rows 2, 4, 14, and 16 (WS): K11, p4, k11.

Rows 3 and 15 (cable row): P11, C4B, p11.

Row 5 (cable row): P4, m1, m3 (k1, p1, k1 all into next st), m1, p4, T4B, T4F, p4, m1, m3, m1, p4—34 sts.

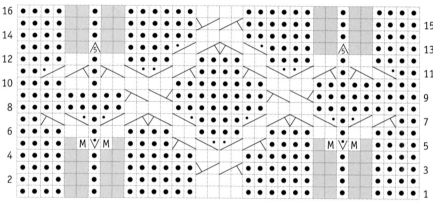

Rows 6 and 12: K4, p2, k1, [p2, k4] 3 times, p2, k1, p2, k4.

Row 7 (cable row): P2, T4B, p1, T4F, T4B, p4, T4F, T4B, p1, T4F, p2.

Rows 8 and 10: K2, p2, k5, p4, k8, p4, k5, p2, k2.

Row 9 (cable row): P2, k2, p5, C4F, p8, C4F, p5, k2, p2.

Row 11 (cable row): P2, T4F, p1, T4B, T4F, p4, T4B, T4F, p1, T4B, p2.

Row 13 (cable row): P4, work 5tog (sl 3 sts pwise wyib, *pass 2nd st on right needle over 1st st and off, sl 1st st on right needle back to left needle, pass 2nd st on left needle over 1st st and off*, sl 1st st on left needle back to right needle; rep from * to * once then purl rem st on left needle) p4, T4F, T4B, p4, work 5 tog, p4—26 sts.

Row 16: Rep row 2.

Rep rows 1–16 for diamonds and circles cable.

Puckered Cable (13-Stitch Panel)

You need two cable needles to work this subtle cable.

9-st Puckered Cable: Sl next 3 sts to 1st cn and hold back, sl following 3 sts to 2nd cn and hold at front, k3 from left needle, k3 from 2nd cn, k3 from 1st cn.

Rows 1, 3, 7, 9, 11, 13, and 15 (RS): P2, k9, p2.

Row 2 and all even rows (WS): K2, p9, k2.

Row 5 (cable row): P2, sl next 3 sts to 1st cn and hold at back, sl following 3 sts to 2nd cn and hold at front, k3 from left needle, k3 from 2nd cn, k3 from 1st cn, p2.

Row 16: Rep row 2.

Rep rows 1–16 for puckered cable.

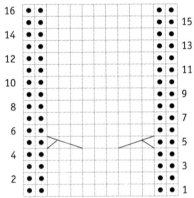

9-st puckered cable

Moss Stitch V Cable
(21-Stitch Panel)

Here's a panel that looks lovely emerging from 2 x 2 ribbing, and framed with plain 4-stitch cables.

3-st RPC: Sl next st onto cn and hold at back, k2 from left needle, p1 from cn.

3-st LPC: Sl next 2 sts onto cn and hold at front, p1 from left needle, k2 from cn.

Row 1 (RS): P2, k2, p4, k2, p1, k2, p4, k2, p2.

Row 2: K8, p2, k1, p2, k8.

Row 3: P8, sl next 3 sts to cn and hold at back, k2 from left needle, place 3rd st from cn back onto left needle and bring cn to front, p1 from left needle, k2 from cn, p8.

Rows 4, 6, 8, 10, 12, 14, and 16: Work sts as they appear.

Row 5: P7, 3-st RPC, k1, 3-st LPC, p8.

Row 7: P6, 3-st RPC, k1, p1, k1, 3-st LPC, p6.

Row 9: P5, 3-st RPC, [k1, p1] twice, k1, 3-st LPC, p5.

Row 11: P4, 3-st RPC, [k1, p1] 3 times, k1, 3-st LPC, p4.

Row 13: P3, 3-st RPC [k1, p1] 4 times, k1, 3-st LPC, p3.

Row 15: P2, 3-st RPC, [k1, p1] 5 times, k1, 3-st LPC, p2.

Rep rows 1–16 for moss stitch V cable.

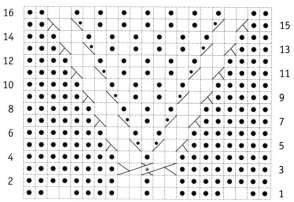

 Sl next 3 sts to cn and hold at back, k2 from left needle, place 3rd st from cn back onto left needle and bring cn to front, p1 from left needle, k2 from cn

Long and Short Cable (10-Stitch Panel)

Here's a variation on the basic 6-stitch cable. You can change the C6B to C6F for a cable that twists to the left. This pattern begins with a wrong side row.

C6B: Sl next 3 sts to cn and hold at back of work, k3 from left needle, k3 from cn.

Row 1 and all odd rows (WS): K2, p6, k2.

Rows 2, 6, 8, 12, 14, 16, and 18 (RS): P2, k6, p2.

Rows 4 and 10 (cable row): P2, C6B, p2.

Row 18: Rep row 2.

Rep rows 1–18 for long and short cable.

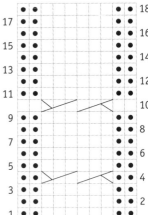

Garter and Stockinette Stitch Cable (14-Stitch Panel)

Here's a pretty cable that you don't see very often.

C10B: Sl next 5 sts to cn and hold at back of work, k5 from left needle, k5 from cn.

Row 1 (RS): P2, k10, p2.

Row 2 (WS): K2, p5, k7.

Rows 3–6: Rep rows 1 and 2 twice.

Row 7 (cable row): P2, C10B, p2.

Row 8: K7, p5, k2.

Row 9: Rep row 1.

Rows 10–16: Rep rows 8 and 9 three more times; then rep row 8 once more.

Row 17 (cable row): Rep row 7.

Rows 18–20: Rep row 2 once; then rep rows 1 and 2 once more.

Rep rows 1–20 for garter and stockinette stitch cable.

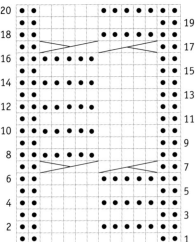

Twisted Taffy Cables

This lively pattern is fitting for baby clothes, kids' knits, and bold women's fashions.

C4B: Sl next 2 sts to cn and hold at back of work, k2 from left needle, k2 from cn.

Cast on a multiple of 22 sts plus 3.

Rows 1, 5, 7, 11, 13, 17, 19, and 23 (RS): P3, *[K8, p3] twice; rep from * to end.

Row 2 and all rows (WS): K3, *[p8, k3] twice; rep from * to end.

Rows 3 and 9: P3, *[C4B] twice, p3, k8, p3; rep from * to end.

Rows 15 and 21: P3, *K8, p3, [C4B] twice, p3; rep from * to end.

Row 24: Rep row 2.

Rep rows 1–24 for twisted taffy cables.

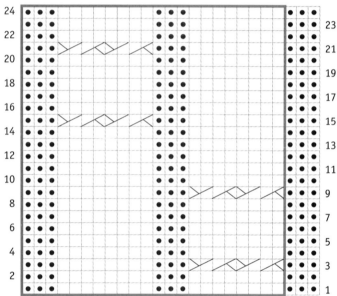

Enclosed Cable (22-Stitch Panel)

This cable is quite fitting for fisherman's knits, socks, and hats.

3-st RPC: Sl next st to cn and hold at back, k2 from left needle, p1 from cn.

3-st LPC: Sl next st to cn and hold at front, k2 from left needle, p1 from cn.

C4F: Sl next 2 sts to cn and hold at front of work, k2 from left needle, k2 from cn.

Row 1 (RS): P7, k8, p7.

Row 2 and all even rows (WS): Work sts as they appear.

Row 3: P6, 3-st RPC, C4F, 3-st LPC, p6.

Row 5: P5, 3-st RPC, p1, k4, p1, 3-st LPC, p5.

Row 7: P4, 3-st RPC, p2, C4F, p2, 3-st LPC, p4.

Row 9: P3, 3-st RPC, p3, k4, p3, 3-st LPC, p3.

Row 11: P2, 3-st RPC, p4, C4F, p4, 3-st LPC, p2.

Row 13: P2, 3-st LPC, p4, k4, p4, 3-st RPC, p2.

Row 15: P3, 3-st LPC, p3, C4F, p3, 3-st RPC, p3.

Row 17: P4, 3-st LPC, p2, k4, p2, 3-st RPC, p4.

Row 19: P5, 3-st LPC, p1, C4F, p1, 3-st RPC, p5.

Row 21: P6, 3-st LPC, k4, 3-st RPC, p6.

Rep rows 1–21 for enclosed cable.

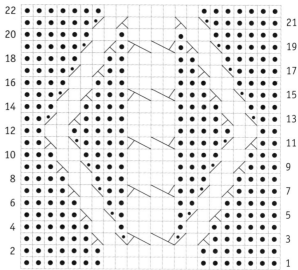

Thick and Thin Diamond Cable (12-Stitch Panel)

Here's a simple yet striking variation on the basic diamond cable. One side of the cable is worked with two stitches, and the other with just one stitch, lending the cable unusual depth and movement. This pattern begins with a wrong side row.

2-st RPC: Sl next st to cn and hold at back, k1 from left needle, p1 from cn.

4-st RPC: Sl next st to cn and hold at back, k3 from left needle, p1 from cn.

2-st LPC: Sl next st to cn and hold at front, p1 from left needle, k1 from cn.

3-st LPC: Sl 2 sts to cn and hold at front, p1 from left needle, k2 from cn.

4-st LPC: Sl next 3 sts to cn and hold at front, p1 from left needle, k3 from cn.

Row 1 (WS): K4, p3, k5.

Row 2 (RS): P4, 4-st RPC, p4.

Row 3 and rem odd rows (WS): Work sts as they appear.

Row 4: P3, 3-st RPC, 2-st LPC, p4.

Row 6: P2, 3-st RPC, p2, 2-st LPC, p3.

Row 8: P1, 3-st RPC, p4, 2-st LPC, p2.

Row 10: P1, 3-st LPC, p4, 2-st RPC, p2.

Row 12: P2, 3-st LPC, p2, 2-st RPC, p3.

Row 14: P3, 3-st LPC, 2-st RPC, p4.

Row 16: P4, 4-st LPC, p4.

Row 18: P4, 2-st RPC, 3-st LPC, p3.

Row 20: P3, 2-st RPC, p2, 3-st LPC, p2.

Row 22: P2, 2-st RPC, p4, 3-st LPC, p1.

Row 24: P1, 2-st LPC, p4, 3-st RPC, p1.

Row 26: P3, 2-st LPC, p2, 3-st RPC, p2.

Row 28: P4, 2-st LPC, 3-st RPC, p3.

Rep rows 1–28 for thick and thin diamond cable.

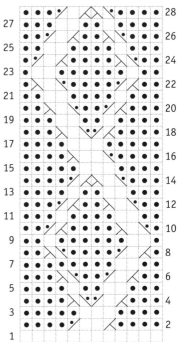

Long and Short Open Cable (16-Stitch Panel)

This pretty cable is long but uncomplicated. It lends a lazy, fluid touch to sweaters, scarves, and throws.

C4B: Sl next 2 sts to cn and hold at back of work, k2 from left needle, k2 from cn.

3-st RPC: Sl next st to cn and hold at back, k2 from left needle, p1 from cn.

3-st LPC: Sl next 2 sts to cn and hold at front, p1 from left needle, k2 from cn.

Rows 1 and 21 (RS): P6, C4B, p6.

Row 2 and all even rows (WS): Work sts as they appear, knitting the sts that were purled on the prev row, and purling the sts that were knit on the prev row.

Rows 3 and 23: P5, 3-st RPC, 3-st LPC, p5.

Rows 5 and 25: P4, 3-st RPC, p2, 3-st LPC, p4.

Row 7: P3, 3-st RPC, p4, 3-st LPC, p3.

Row 9: P2, 3-st RPC, p6, 3-st LPC, p2.

Row 11: P2, k2, p8, k2, p2.

Row 13: P2, 3-st LPC, p6, 3-st RPC, p2.

Row 15: P3, 3-st LPC, p4, 3-st RPC, p3.

Rows 17 and 29: P4, 3-st LPC, p2, 3-st RPC, p4.

Rows 19 and 31: P5, 3-st LPC, 3-st RPC, p5.

Row 27: P4, [k2, p4] twice.

Row 32: K6, p4, k6.

Rep rows 1–32 for long and short open cable.

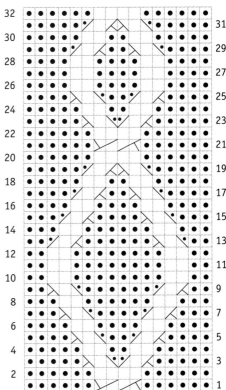

Serpentine Cable with Bobbles (12-Stitch Panel)

Here is a unique variation on the bobbled cable. This pattern begins with a wrong side row.

T4F: Sl next 2 sts to cn and hold at front, p2 from left needle, k2 from cn.

T4B: Sl next 2 sts onto cn and hold at back, k2 from left needle, p2 from cn.

3-st LPC: Sl next 2 sts to dpn and hold at front, p1 from left needle, k2 from dpn.

3-st RPC: Sl 1 st to dpn and hold at back, k2 from left needle, p1 from dpn.

Mb (make bobble): Knit into front, back, front, back, and front of next st; without turning work, use left needle to pass 2nd st over 1st st and off right needle 4 times.

C4B: Sl next 2 sts to cn and hold at back of work, k2 from left needle, k2 from cn.

C4F: Sl next 2 sts to cn and hold at front of work, k2 from left needle, k2 from cn.

Rows 1, 3, 21, and 23 (WS): K2, p2, k4, p2, k2.

Rows 2 and 22 (RS): P2, k2, p4, k2, p2.

Rows 4 and 24: P2, T4F, T4B, p2.

Rows 5, 19, 25, and 39: K4, p4, k4.

Row 6: P4, T4F, p4.

Rows 7 and 17: K4, p2, k6.

Row 8: P6, 3-st LPC, p3.

Rows 9 and 15: K3, p2, k7.

Row 10: P7, 3-st LPC, p2.

Rows 11 and 13: K2, p2, k8.

Row 12: P3, mb, p4, k2, p2.

Row 14: P7, 3-st RPC, p2.

Row 16: P6, 3-st RPC, p3.

Row 18: P4, C4B, p4.

Row 20: P2, T4B, T4F, p2.

Row 26: P4, T4B, p4.

Rows 27 and 37: K6, p2, k4.

Row 28: P3, 3-st RPC, p6.

Rows 29 and 35: K7, p2, k3.

Row 30: P2, 3-st RPC, p7.

Rows 31 and 33: K8, p2, k2.

Row 32: P2, k2, p4, mb, p3.

Row 34: P2, 3-st LPC, p7.

Row 36: P3, 3-st LPC, p6.

Row 38: P4, C4F, p4.

Row 40: P2, T4B, T4F, p2.

Rep rows 1–40 for serpentine cable with bobbles.

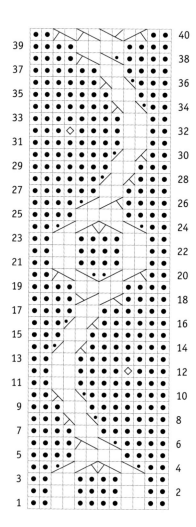

CHAPTER 7

Drop-stitch, Yarn Overs, Eyelet, and Lace

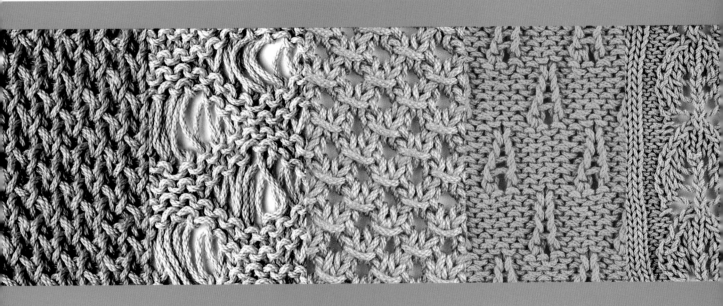

Mesh Pattern

Repeat the same row for this easy and versatile pattern. It looks great in both fine and bulky yarns.

Sl 1-k1-psso (skp): Sl 1, k1, pass sl st over the k1.

Cast on an even number of sts.

Row 1 (RS): K1, *yo, sl 1-k1-psso; rep from * to last st, k1.

Row 2 (WS): Rep row 1.

Rep rows 1 and 2 for mesh pattern.

Lace Rib

This easy and pretty pattern works wonderfully for wraps, dresses, and baby clothes.

Cast on a multiple of 3 sts plus 1.

Row 1 (RS): K1, *yo, ssk, k1; rep from * to end.

Row 2 (WS): K1, *yo, p2tog, k1; rep from * to end.

Rep rows 1 and 2 for lace rib.

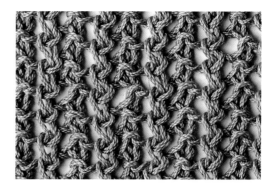

Train Tracks

What's nice about this pattern is that, unlike so many openwork patterns that use yarn overs paired with knit 2 togethers, it doesn't cause the fabric to slant in one direction. Train tracks works beautifully for scarves or as a lace panel inserted into summer cardigans, coverlets, and more.

Cast on a multiple of 4 sts.

Row 1 (RS): *K2tog, [yo] twice, ssk; rep from * to end.

Row 2 (WS): *K1, [k1, p1] into the 2 yos, k1; rep from * to end.

Rep rows 1 and 2 for train tracks.

Oversized Eyelet Lace

This pattern is unusual in that it is a 3-row repeat. There is no "right side." The third row, a knit row, must be worked with a needle 3 to 4 sizes larger than the size your yarn calls for, in order to keep it loose. Your stitch count will decrease on row 1 and return to the original number on row 2.

Cast on multiples of 8 sts.

Row 1: P2, *yo, p4tog; rep from * to last 2 sts, p2.

Row 2: K2, *k1, (k1, p1, k1) into yo from prev row; rep from * to last 2 sts, k2.

Row 3: Using a needle 3–4 sizes larger, knit.

Rep rows 1–3 for oversized eyelet lace.

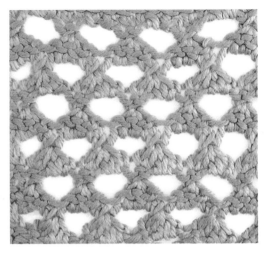

Drop Stitch Garter

This easy drop stitch pattern makes wonderful scarves, throws, and shawls.

Cast on any number of sts.

Row 1 (RS): Knit.

Row 2 (WS): Knit.

Row 3: K1, *yo twice, k1; rep from * to end.

Row 4: Knit across, dropping the yarn overs as you go.

Rep rows 1–4 for drop stitch garter pattern.

Triangle Lace

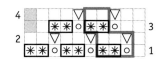

This very textured lace pattern is great for baby blankets, throws, and scarves.

Cast on an odd number of sts.

Row 1 (RS): K1, *yo, sl 1, k1, yo, psso the knit st and the yo; rep from * to end.

Row 2 (WS): *P2, drop yo from prev row; rep from * to last st, p1.

Row 3: K2, *yo, sl 1, k1, yo, psso the knit st and the yo; rep from * to last st, k1.

Row 4: P3, *drop yo from prev row, p2; rep from * to end.

Rep rows 1–4 for triangle lace.

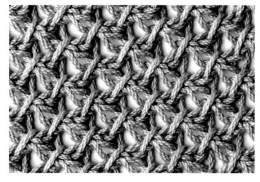

✳✳ Sl 1, k1, yo, psso the knit st and the yo

Cell Stitch

This easy and very open eyelet pattern makes great scarves and throws. Note that the first row is a wrong-side row.

Cast on a multiple of 3 sts.

Rows 1 and 3 (WS): Purl.

Row 2 (RS): K2, *k2tog, yo, k1; rep from * to last st, k1.

Row 4: K2, *yo, k1, k2tog; rep from * to last st, k1.

Rep rows 1–4 for cell stitch.

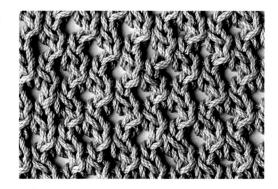

Brioche Honeycomb

Brioche patterns combine yarn overs with slipped stitches and knit 2 togethers (or purl 2 togethers), and the result is usually a loose but three-dimensional fabric. Going up a needle size gives this pattern a nice, soft drape. This pattern begins with a wrong side row.

Cast on an even number of sts.

Row 1 (WS): *Yo, sl 1 wyib, k1; rep from * to end.

Row 2 (RS): *K1, k2tog (these are the yo and the slipped st from the prev row); rep from * to end.

Row 3: K1, *yo, sl 1 wyib, k1; rep from * to last st, k1.

Row 4: K2, *k2tog, k1; rep from * to end.

Rep rows 1–4 for brioche honeycomb.

Openwork Rows

This four-row pattern looks almost like a grid of openwork. It's simple to work and is fitting for large expanses of fabric.

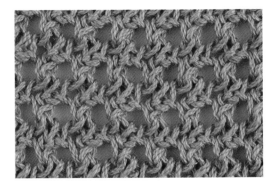

M1 pwise: Left horizontal strand of yarn between sts with left needle and purl it.

Cast on an odd number of sts.

Row 1 (RS): Purl.

Row 2 (WS): *P2tog; rep from * to last st, p1.

Row 3: P1, *M1 pwise, p1; rep from * to end.

Row 4: P1, *yo, p2tog; rep from * to end.

Rep rows 1–4 for openwork rows.

Zigzag Lace

Here's a lively openwork pattern that works up over only four rows.

Sl 1-k1-psso (skp): Sl 1, k1, pass sl st over the k1.

Sl 1-k2tog-psso (sk2p): Sl 1, k2tog, pass sl st over the k2tog.

Cast on a multiple of 6 sts plus 1.

Row 1 (RS): K1, *yo, sl 1-k1-psso, k1, k2tog, yo, k1; rep from * to end.

Row 2 (WS): Purl.

Row 3: K2, *yo, sl 1-k2tog-psso, yo, k3; rep from * to last 5 sts, yo, sl 1-k2tog-psso, yo, k2.

Row 4: Rep row 2.

Rep rows 1–4 for zigzag lace.

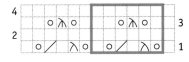

Diagonal Lace

This simple lace is lovely for baby clothes and summer cardigans. This pattern uses the decrease slip, slip, knit.

Cast on a multiple of 6 sts.

Row 1 (RS): *[K1, yo, ssk] twice; rep from * to end.

Rows 2 and 4 (WS): Purl.

Row 3: *K2, yo, ssk, k2; rep from * to end.

Row 5: *K3, yo, ssk, k1; rep from * to end.

Row 6: Rep row 2.

Rep rows 1–6 for diagonal lace.

Yarn Over Stripe

This easy openwork pattern repeats as a horizontal stripe.

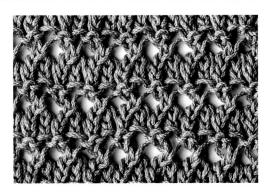

Cast on any number of sts.

Row 1 (RS): K1, *yo, k1; rep from * to last st, k1.

Row 2 (WS): K1, purl across to last st, k1.

Row 3: K1, *k2tog; rep from * to last st, k1.

Rows 4 and 5: K1, *yo, k2tog; rep from * to last st, k1.

Row 6: Knit.

Rep rows 1–6 for yarn over stripe pattern.

Stockinette Drop Stitch

This pattern is easy and looks very elegant. Use it with a knit-in border, or vary the number of stockinette stitch rows or the number of yarn overs for an alternate version.

Cast on any number of sts.

Rows 1 and 5 (RS): Knit.

Rows 2 and 6 (WS): Purl.

Row 3: K1, *yo twice, k1; rep from * to end of row.

Row 4: Purl across, dropping yo loops as you go.

Rep rows 1–6 for stockinette drop stitch.

Ridge and Eyelet Stitch

This eyelet pattern forms a simple yet pleasing three-dimensional fabric. The rows between the eyelets are raised, creating a wavy effect.

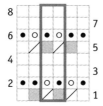

Cast on an even number of sts.

Rows 1 and 5 (RS): K1, *k2tog; rep from * to last st, k1.

Row 2 (WS): K2, *yo, k1; rep from * to end.

Rows 3 and 7: Knit.

Row 4: Purl.

Row 6: *K1, yo; rep from * to last 2 sts, k2.

Row 8: Rep row 4.

Rep rows 1–8 for ridge and eyelet stitch.

Seafoam Pattern

This drop stitch pattern is great for scarves, wraps, shawls, and baby blankets.

Cast on a multiple of 10 sts plus 6.

Row 1 (RS): Knit.

Row 2 (WS): Knit.

Row 3: K6, *yo twice, k1, yo 3 times, k1, yo 4 times, k1, yo 3 times, k1, yo twice, k6; rep from * to end.

Rows 4 and 8: Knit across, dropping yo loops as you go.

Rows 5 and 6: Knit.

Row 7: K1, *yo twice, k1, yo 3 times, k1, yo 4 times, k1, yo 3 times, k1, yo twice, k6; rep from * across, ending last rep k1.

Rep rows 1–8 for seafoam pattern.

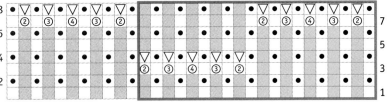

Eyelet Chevrons

This simple pattern is perfect for scarves, shoulder wraps, and table cloths.

Sl 1-k1-psso (skp): Sl 1, k1, pass sl st over the k1.

Cast on a multiple of 9 sts.

Row 1 (RS): *K4, yo, sl 1-k1-psso, k3; rep from * to end.

Rows 2, 4, and 6 (WS): Purl.

Row 3: *K2, k2tog, yo, k1, yo, sl 1-k1-psso, k2; rep from * to end.

Row 5: *K1, k2tog, yo, k3, yo, sl 1-k1-psso, k1; rep from * to end.

Row 7: *K2tog, yo, k5, yo, sl 1-k1-psso; rep from * to end.

Row 8: Purl.

Rep rows 1–8 for eyelet chevrons.

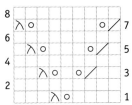

Fishtail Lace

This elegant pattern leaves a pointed border at the hem, so it can be used both as a border and an allover pattern. It's perfect for summer tank tops and wraps.

Sl 1-k2tog-psso (sk2p): sl 1, k2tog, pass sl st over the k2tog.

Cast on a multiple of 10 sts.

Row 1 (RS): *Yo, k3, sl 1-k2tog-psso, k3, yo, k1; rep from * to end.

Row 2 (WS): Purl.

Row 3: *K1, yo, k2, sl 1-k2tog-psso, k2, yo, k1, p1; rep from * to end.

Rows 4 and 6: *K1, p9; rep from * to end.

Row 5: *K2, yo, k1, sl 1-k2tog-psso, k1, yo, k2, p1; rep from * end.

Row 7: *K3, yo, sl 1-k2tog-psso, yo, k3, p1; rep from * to end.

Row 8: Purl.

Rep rows 1–8 for fishtail lace.

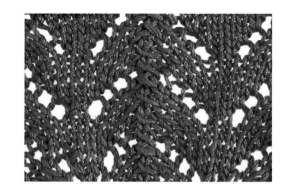

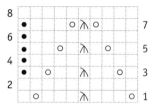

Knotted Eyelets

This pattern is easy to work, and the result is a fancy textured stitch that looks great for babies', girls', and women's knits.

Cast on a multiple of 3 sts.

Row 1 (RS): K2, *yo, [k3, pass the first of these 3 knit sts over last 2 sts just worked]; rep from * to last st, k1.

Rows 2 and 4 (WS): Purl.

Row 3: K1, *[k3, pass the first of these 3 knit sts over last 2 sts just worked], yo; rep from * to last 2 sts, k2.

Rep rows 1–4 for knotted eyelets.

Falling Rain

This eyelet pattern is worked on a background of reverse stockinette stitch.

Cast on a multiple of 6 sts.

Row 1 (RS): *P4, yo, p2tog; rep from * to end.

Rows 2, 4, and 6 (WS): K1, *p1, k5; rep from * to last 5 sts, p1, k4.

Rows 3 and 5: P4, *k1, p5; rep from * to last 2 sts, k1, p1.

Row 7: P1, *yo, p2tog, p4; rep from * to last 5 sts, yo, p2tog, p3.

Rows 8 and 10: K4, *p1, k5; rep from * to last 2 sts, p1, k1.

Rows 9 and 11: P1, *k1, p5; rep from * to last 5 sts, k1, p4.

Row 12: Rep row 8.

Rep rows 1–12 for falling rain.

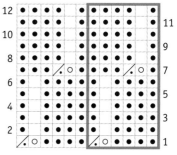

Overlapping Lace

It's hard to believe that repeating just ten rows can create such a beautiful pattern. You can use this stitch for all kinds of knits.

Sl 1-k1-psso (skp): Sl 1, k1, pass sl st over the k1.

Cast on a multiple of 6 sts plus 4.

Row 1 (RS): K2, *yo, sl 1-k1-psso, k4; rep from * to last 2 sts, yo, sl 1-k1-psso.

Row 2 and all even rows (WS): Purl.

Row 3: K2, *yo, k1, sl 1-k1-psso, k3; rep from * to last 2 sts, yo, sl 1-k1-psso.

Row 5: K2, *yo, k2, sl 1-k1-psso, k2; rep from * to last 2 sts, yo, sl 1-k1-psso.

Row 7: K2, *yo, k3, sl 1-k1-psso, k1; rep from * to last 2 sts, yo, sl 1-k1-psso.

Row 9: K2, *yo, k4, sl 1-k1-psso; rep from * to last 2 sts, yo, sl 1-k1-psso.

Row 10: Purl.

Rep rows 1–10 for overlapping lace.

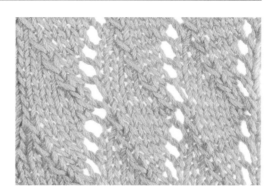

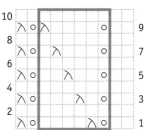

Arrowhead Lace

This lace pattern is easy to follow and works well in a shawl or throw. It begins with a wrong side row.

Sl 1-k2tog-psso (sk2p): sl 1, k2tog, pass sl st over the k2tog.

Cast on a multiple of 6 sts plus 1.

Row 1 and all odd rows (WS): Purl.

Row 2 (RS): K3, *yo, ssk, k4; rep from * to last 4 sts, yo, ssk, k2.

Row 4: K1, *k2tog, yo, k1, yo, ssk, k1; rep from * to end.

Row 6: K2tog, yo, *k3, yo, sl 1-k2tog-psso, yo; rep from * to last 5 sts, k3, yo, ssk.

Rows 8 and 10: K1, *yo, ssk, k1, k2tog, yo, k1; rep from * to end.

Rep rows 1–10 for arrowhead lace.

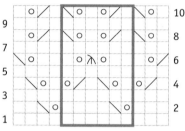

Acorn Lace

This is an unusual pattern that looks like upside-down acorns, complete with caps. It is suitable for bedspreads and baby blankets.

Cast on a multiple of 6 sts plus 2.

Rows 1 and 3 (RS): K4, *p3, k3; rep from *, ending last rep with k1 instead of k3.

Row 2 and all even rows (WS): Work sts as they appear.

Row 5: K1, *yo, k3tog, yo, k3; rep from * to last st, k1.

Row 7: K1, *p3, k3; rep from * to last st, k1.

Row 9: K4, *yo, k3tog, yo, k3; rep from *, ending last rep with k1 instead of k3.

Row 10: Purl.

Rep rows 3–10 for acorn lace.

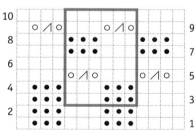

Triple Rib Mock Cable with Eyelets (36-Stitch Panel)

You can separate the mirror image mock cables in this pattern for cardigans or to frame a special center panel. It begins with a wrong side row.

Sl 1-k2tog-psso (sk2p): Sl 1, k2tog, pass sl st over k2tog.

Row 1 (WS): K7, [p1, k1] twice, p1, k12, [p1, k1] twice, p1, k7.

Row 2 (RS): K6, k2tog, [p1, k1] twice, yo, k12, yo, [k1, p1] twice, ssk, k6.

Row 3: K6, [p1, k1] twice, p3, k10, p3, [k1, p1] twice, k6.

Row 4: K5, k2tog, [p1, k1] twice, yo, k1, yo, ssk, k8, k2tog, [yo, k1] twice, p1, k1, p1, ssk, k5.

Row 5: K5, [p1, k1] twice, p3, k1, p1, k8, p1, k1, p3, [k1, p1] twice, k5.

Row 6: K4, k2tog, [p1, k1] twice, [yo, k1] twice, p1, ssk, k6, k2tog, p1, k1, [yo, k1] twice, p1, k1, p1, ssk, k4.

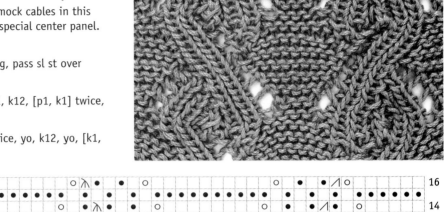

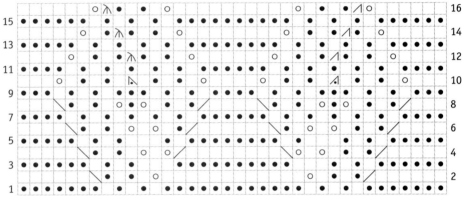

Rows 7 and 11: K4, [p1, k1] 5 times, p1, k6, [p1, k1] 5 times, p1, k4.

Row 8: K3, k2tog, [p1, k1] twice, yo, p1, yo, [k1, p1] twice, ssk, k4, k2tog, [p1, k1] twice, yo, p1, yo, [k1, p1] twice, ssk, k3.

Row 9: K3, [p1, k1] twice, p1, k3, [p1, k1] twice, p1, k4, [p1, k1] twice, p1, k3, [p1, k1] twice, p1, k3.

Row 10: K3, yo, [k1, p1] twice, k1, p3tog, [k1, p1] twice, k1, yo, k4, yo, [k1, p1] twice, k1, p3tog tbl, [k1, p1] twice, k1, yo, k3.

Row 12: K4, yo, [k1, p1] twice, k3tog, [p1, k1] twice, yo, k6, yo, [k1, p1] twice, sl 1-k2tog-psso, [p1, k1] twice, yo, k4.

Row 13: K5, [p1, k1] 4 times, p1, k8, [p1, k1] 4 times, p1, k5.

Row 14: K5, yo, k1, p1, k3tog, [p1, k1] twice, yo, k8, yo, [k1, p1] twice, sl 1-k2tog-psso, p1, k1, yo, k5.

Row 15: K6, [p1, k1] 3 times, p1, k10, [p1, k1] 3 times, p1, k6.

Row 16: K6, yo, k3tog, [p1, k1] twice, yo, k10, yo, [k1, p1] twice, sl 1-k2tog-psso, yo, k6.

Rep rows 1–16 for triple rib mock cable with eyelets.

Snowflake Band

This eyelet pattern works well as a decorative border along a hem or cuff, or it can be repeated as an allover pattern. It uses the sl 2-k1-p2sso double decrease, and begins with a wrong side row.

Sl 2-k1-p2sso (s2kp): Slip the 1st and 2nd sts tog kwise, k1, pass the 2 sl sts over the knit stitch.

Cast on a multiple of 8 sts plus 5.

Row 1 (WS): Knit.

Rows 2 and 10 (RS): Knit.

Rows 3, 5, 7, and 9: Purl.

Rows 4 and 8: K4, *k2tog, yo, k1, yo, k2tog, k3; rep from * to last st, k1.

Row 6: K5, *yo, sl 2-k1-p2sso, yo, k5; rep from * to end.

Rep rows 1–10 for snowflake band.

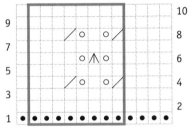

Lace Leaf (9-Stitch Panel)

This panel works well as an accent. Try it on throws or centered on sleeves.

Sl 2-k1-p2sso (s2kp): Slip the 1st and 2nd sts tog kwise, k1, pass the 2 sl sts over the knit stitch.

Row 1 (RS): P3, [k1, yo] twice, k1, p3.

Rows 2 and 8 (WS): K3, p5, k3.

Row 3: P3, k2, yo, k1, yo, k2, p3.

Rows 4 and 6: K3, p7, k3.

Row 5: P3, ssk, k1, [yo, k1] twice, k2tog, p3.

Row 7: P3, ssk, k3, k2tog, p3.

Row 9: P3, ssk, k1, k2tog, p3.

Row 10: K3, p3, k3.

Row 11: P3, yo, sl 2-k1-p2sso, yo, p3.

Row 12: Rep row 10.

Rep rows 1–12 for lace leaf panel.

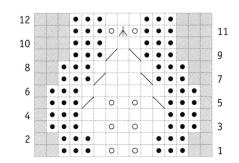

Trefoil Lace

Delicate trefoils on a background of reverse stockinette stitch form this easy-to-work pattern.

Sl 1-k2tog-psso (sk2p): Sl 1, k2tog, pass sl st over k2tog.

Cast on a multiple of 8 sts plus 5.

Rows 1, 3, 5, 9, and 11 (RS): Purl.

Row 2 (WS): K5, *yo, sl 1- k2tog-psso, yo, k5; rep from * to end.

Rows 4, 6, 10, and 12: Knit.

Row 7: P6, *insert right needle into st 4 rows below next st and knit it, drop corresponding unworked st from left needle and allow sts below to unravel down to worked st (making the long st at the top of the trefoil), p7; rep from *, ending last rep p6.

Row 8: K1, *yo, sl 1-k2tog-psso, yo, k5; rep from *, ending last rep k1.

Row 13: P2, *insert right needle into st 4 rows below next st and knit it, drop corresponding unworked st from left needle and allow sts below to unravel down to worked st (making the long st at the top of the trefoil), p7; rep from *, ending last rep p2.

Rep rows 2–13 for trefoil lace.

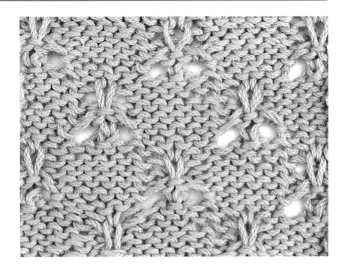

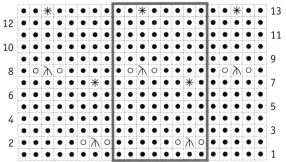

Flower Lace

This stitch works well as an allover pattern on summer cardigans and shawls.

Cast on a multiple of 8 sts.

Rows 1 and 9 (RS): Knit.

Rows 2, 4, 6, 8, 10, 12, and 14 (WS): Purl.

Rows 3 and 7: K3, *yo, ssk, k6; rep from *, ending last rep k3.

Row 5: K1, *k2tog, yo, k1, yo, ssk, k3; rep from * to last 2 sts, k2.

Rows 11 and 15: K7, *yo, ssk, k6; rep from * to last st, k1.

Row 13: K5, *k2tog, yo, k1, yo, ssk, k3; rep from * to last 3 sts, k3.

Row 16: Purl.

Rep rows 1–16 for flower lace.

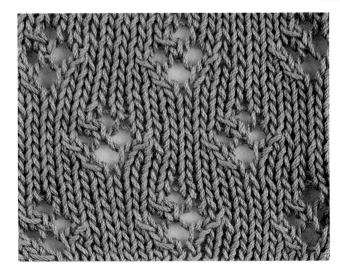

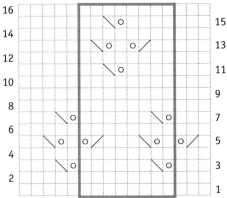

Bellflower Lace

Don't be put off by the seeming complexity of this beautiful lace. After you work a few repeats, you'll be able to work the pattern without having to read.

Sl 1-k1-psso (skp): Sl 1, k1, pass sl st over the k1.

Sl 1-k2tog-psso (sk2p): Sl 1, k2tog, pass sl st over k2tog.

Sl 1-k3tog-psso (sk3p): Sl 1, k3tog, pass sl st over k3tog.

Cast on a multiple of 17 sts plus 2.

Row 1 (RS): P2, *yo, k2tog, yo, [k2tog] 3 times, k2, yo, k3, yo, sl 1-k1-psso, yo, p2; rep from * to end.

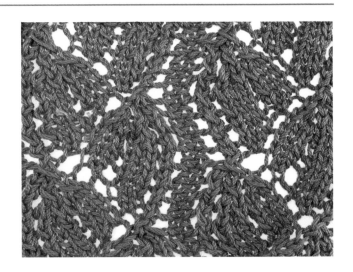

Row 2 and all even rows (WS): Work sts as they appear.

Row 3: P2, *yo, k2tog, [k3tog] twice, yo, k1, yo, k2, [sl 1-k1-psso, yo] twice, p2; rep from * to end.

Row 5: P2, *yo, k4tog, yo, k3, yo, k2, [sl 1-k1-psso, yo] twice, p2; rep from * to end.

Row 7: P2, *yo, k2tog, yo, k1, yo, k2, sl 1-k1-psso, yo, k2, [sl 1-k1-psso, yo] twice, p2; rep from * to end.

Row 9: P2, *yo, k2tog, yo, k3, yo, k2, [sl 1-k1-psso] twice, [sl 1-k1-psso, yo] twice, p2; rep from * to end.

Row 11: P2, *[yo, k2tog] twice, k2, yo, k1, yo, [sl 1-k2tog-psso] twice, sl 1-k1-psso, yo, p2; rep from * to end.

Row 13: P2, *[yo, k2tog] twice, k2, yo, k3, yo, sl 1-k3tog-psso, yo, p2; rep from * to end.

Row 15: P2, *[yo, k2tog] twice, k2, yo, sl 1-k1-psso, k2, yo, k1, yo, sl 1-k1-psso, yo, p2; rep from * to end.

Row 16: Rep row 2.

Rep rows 1–16 for bellflower lace.

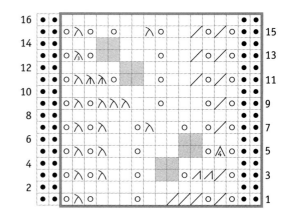

Lace Checks

Perfect for baby blankets and bedspreads, lace checks is an easy-to-work pattern. It begins with a wrong side row.

Sl 1-k1-psso (skp): Sl 1, k1, pass sl st over the k1.

Cast on a multiple of 16 sts.

Row 1 and all odd rows (WS): Purl.

Rows 2, 4, 6, and 8 (RS): *K8, [yo, sl 1-k1-psso] 4 times; rep from * to end.

Rows 10, 12, 14, and 16: *[Yo, sl 1-k1-psso] 4 times, k8; rep from * to end.

Rep rows 1–16 for lace checks.

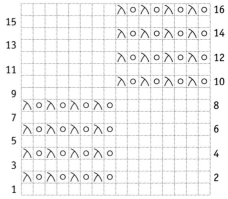

Candlelight Lace

The paired increases and decreases of this pattern create the look of a radiating glow around the open-work.

Sl 1-k1-psso (skp): Sl 1, k1, pass sl st over the k1.

Cast on a multiple of 14 sts plus 1.

Rows 1, 3, 11, and 13 (RS): Knit.

Row 2 and all even rows (WS): Work sts as they appear.

Rows 5, 7, and 9: P1, *yo, k4, sl 1-k1-psso, p1, k2tog, k4, yo, p1; rep from * to end.

Rows 15, 17, and 19: P1, *k2tog, k4, yo, p1, yo, k4, sl 1-k1-psso, p1; rep from * to end.

Row 20: Rep row 2.

Rep rows 1–20 for candlelight lace.

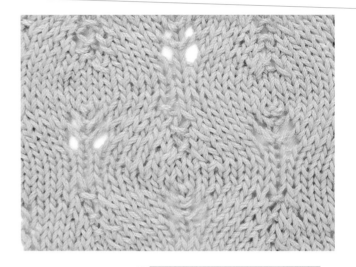

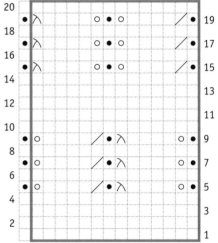

Many Circles Lace

Here's an unusual lace that is lovely for light wraps, tablecloths, and bedskirts. And it looks just as beautiful on the "wrong side."

Sl 1-k2tog-psso (sk2p): Sl 1, k2tog, pass sl st over k2tog.

Sl 2-k1-p2sso (s2kp): Slip the 1st and 2nd sts tog kwise, k1, pass the 2 sl sts over the knit stitch.

RLI (right lifted increase): Inc 1 by knitting tbl into st below 1st st on left needle, then knit the st above as usual.

Cast on a multiple of 12 sts plus 3.

Row 1 (RS): K1, k2tog, *yo, k2tog, yo, p5, yo, ssk, yo, sl 1-k2tog-psso; rep from *, ending last rep ssk, k1.

Row 2 (WS): P5, *k5, p7; rep from * to last 10 sts, k5, p5.

Row 3: K1, *yo, k3tog, yo, p7, yo, ssk; rep from * to last 2 sts, yo, k2tog.

Rows 4, 6, and 8: P4, *k7, p5; rep from * to last 11 sts, k7, p4.

Row 5: Ssk, yo, *ssk, yo, p7, yo, sl 1-k2tog-psso, yo; rep from * to last st, k1.

Row 7: K1, *yo, sl 2-k1-p2sso, yo, p7, yo, k2tog; rep from * to last 2 sts, k2tog.

Row 9: K1, RLI, *yo, ssk, yo, p2tog, p3tog, p2tog, yo, k2tog, yo, kfbf; rep from *, ending last rep LRI, k1.

NOTE: Use the instructions for "RLI" for all future *single* increases.

Row 10: P6, *k3tog, p9; rep from * to last 9 sts, k3tog, p6.

Row 11: K1, RLI, *[yo, ssk] twice, p1, [k2tog, yo] twice, kfbf; rep from *, ending last rep RLI, k1.

Row 12: P7, *k1, p11; rep from * to last 8 sts, k1, p7.

Row 13: K1, p3, *yo, ssk, yo, sl 1-k2tog-psso, yo, k2tog, yo, p5; rep from *, ending last rep p3, k1.

Row 14: P1, k3, *p7, k5; rep from * to last 11 sts, p7, k3, p1.

Row 15: K1, p4, *yo, ssk, yo, k3tog, yo, p7; rep from *, ending last rep p4, k1.

Rows 16, 18, and 20: P1, k4, *p5, k7; rep from * to last 10 sts, p5, k4, p1.

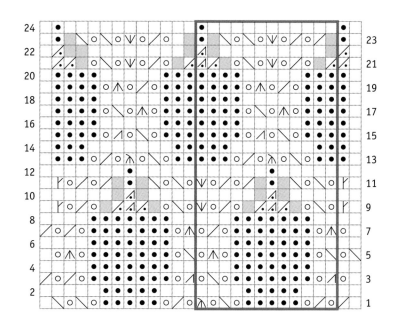

Row 17: K1, p4, *yo, sl 2-k1-p2sso, yo, ssk, yo, p7; rep from *, ending last rep p4, k1.

Row 19: K1, p4, *yo, k2tog, yo, sl 2-k1-p2sso, yo, p7; rep from *, ending last rep p4, k1.

Row 21: K1, p2tog, *p2tog, yo, k2tog, yo, kfbf, yo, ssk, yo, p2tog, p3tog; rep from *, ending last rep p2tog, k1.

Row 22: P1, k2tog, *p9, k3tog; rep from * to last 12 sts, p9, k2tog, p1.

Row 23: K1, p1, *[k2tog, yo] twice, kfbf, [yo, ssk] twice, p1; rep from * to last st, k1.

Row 24: P1, k1, *p11, k1; rep from * to last st, p1.

Rep rows 1–24 for many circles lace.

CHAPTER 8

Borders and Edgings

Easy Eyelet Border

This is a simple yet versatile border pattern. Use it for sleeves, skirts, hats, and blankets.

Cast on an even number of sts.

Rows 1–4: Knit.

Row 5: K1, *yo, k2tog; rep from * to last st, k1.

Rows 6–8: Knit.

NOTE: You can lengthen the border by working an inch or so of stockinette stitch after row 8 and repeat rows 1–8 for a second band.

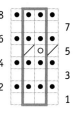

Basic Ruffle

For this ruffle, you need to start with twice the number of stitches as there are in the main part of your knitting. For example, if you are knitting a sweater back over 60 stitches, you cast on 120 stitches for this ruffle.

Work in St st to the desired length of the ruffle, ending with a purl row.

K2tog across the entire row. You end up with half the number of sts you cast on.

NOTE: You can work 3 rows of garter stitch to accentuate the decrease row. The chart is for reference only; adjust the number of rows to your project.

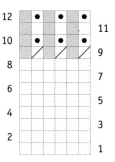

Curly Ruffle

This fun ruffle looks great on baby blankets and little girls' sweaters. You need to cast on four times the number of stitches you want to end up with, minus 3. For example, if you want to end up with 60 stitches, you cast on 237 stitches to create a curly ruffle.

Row 1 (RS): K1, *k2, pass the first of these 2 sts over the second and off the needle; rep from * to end of row.

Row 2 (WS): P1, *p2tog; rep from * to end of row.

NOTE: You can work the ruffle on smaller needles if you want it to be tighter.

Bobbled Border

This border adds a simple yet substantial, three-dimensional edge to hems and cuffs. It begins with a wrong side row.

Mb (make bobble): Knit into the front, back, front, back, and front (that's five times) of the next stitch. Without turning the work, use the left needle to pick up the fourth stitch and pass it over the fifth and off the needle; pass the third over the fifth and off; pass the second over the fifth and off; and finally, pass the first over the fifth stitch and off.

Cast on a multiple of 6 sts plus 5.

Row 1 (WS): Knit.

Row 2 (RS—bobble row): K2, *mb, k5; rep from * to last 3 sts, mb, k2.

Rows 3–5: Knit.

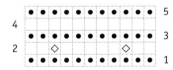

Chevron Edging

Pairing decreases and increases will produce the pointed edges in this pattern. For variation, you can increase the number of stitches between the decrease and the increase.

Cast on a multiple of 11 sts.

Rows 1–2: Knit.

Row 3 (RS): *K2tog, k3, M1R, k1, M1L, k3, k2tog tbl; rep from * to end.

Row 4: Purl.

Rep rows 3–4 to desired length.

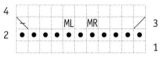

Scallop and Eyelet Edging

This edging is similar to the chevron edging, but uses yarn overs instead of M1s for the increases.

Cast on a multiple of 11 sts.

Rows 1, 3, and 5 (RS): Purl.

Rows 2, 4, and 6: Knit.

Row 7: *K2tog, k3, yo, k1, yo, k3, k2tog; rep from * to end.

Row 8: K2, purl to last 2 sts, k2.

Rep rows 7–8 to desired length.

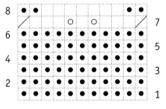

Easy Pointed Edging

This border creates a series of diagonally biased points. You make the border as long as the edge you need to attach it to and sew it on later.

Cast on 6 sts.

Row 1 (RS): K3, yo, k3—7 sts.

Rows 2, 4, 6, 8, and 10 (WS): Knit.

Row 3: K3, yo, k4—8 sts.

Row 5: K3, yo, k5—9 sts.

Row 7: K3, yo, k6—10 sts.

Row 9: K3, yo, k7—11 sts.

Row 11: K3, yo, k8—12 sts.

Row 12: BO 6 sts, k5—6 sts.

Rep rows 1–12 until the edging is the desired length. BO all stitches.

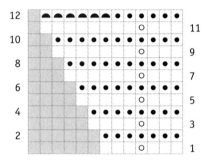

Serrated Lace Edging

This lacy edging is worked sideways as a separate piece. You cast on 11 stitches, then repeat the four rows over and over until the edging is the same length as the edge you will be attaching it to. Binding off the first 4 stitches on row 4 is what creates the serrated edge.

Cast on 11 sts.

Knit one row in preparation for beginning the pattern.

Row 1 (RS): K3, [yo, ssk, k1] twice, [yo] twice, k1, [yo] twice, k1—15 sts.

NOTE: Treat the double yarn overs as 2 stitches.

Row 2 (WS): [K2, p1] 4 times, k3.

Row 3: K3, yo, ssk, k1, yo, ssk, k7.

Row 4: BO 4 sts, k3, p1, k2, p1, k3—11 sts.

Rep rows 1–4 to desired length.

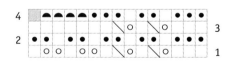

Ribbed Lace Trim

You can use this pretty edging for cuffs, summery sweaters, and wraps. It would also look lovely sewn onto curtain hems and pillowcases. If using the trim for cuffs or other knit items, you can continue with the knitting of that item from where you leave off with the trim; just remember to cast on one-third more stitches than you need to end up with.

Cast on a multiple of 3 sts plus 1.

Row 1 (RS): K1 tbl, *p2, k1 tbl; rep from * to end.

Row 2: P1, *k1 tbl, k1, p1; rep from * to end.

Rep rows 1 and 2 until trim is required length, ending on row 2.

Next row (RS): K1 tbl, *drop next st, p1, k1 tbl; rep from * to end.

NOTE: dropping the stitches is what will make the ladders between the ribs.

With the new stitch count, work 4–6 rows of ribbing as follows:

Row 1 (WS): P1, *k1 tbl, p1; rep from * to end.

Row 2: K1 tbl, *p1, k1 tbl; rep from * to end.

Unravel dropped sts to the CO row.

NOTE: Use the chart for reference only—the number of rows you work for the ladder section and the rib section is up to you.

If using the trim as a separate edging (to be sewn on), BO sts; otherwise, continue from here with your pattern.

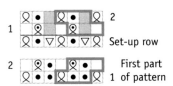

Tailfin Edging

This pointed edging works wonderfully as a trim on girls' sweaters, baby blankets, or repeated as a scarf pattern.

Mb (make bobble): Knit into the front, back, front, back, and front of the next stitch. Without turning the work, use the left needle to pick up the fourth stitch and pass it over the fifth and off the needle; pass the third over the fifth and off; pass the second over the fifth and off; and finally, pass the first over the fifth stitch and off.

Sl 1-k2tog-psso (sk2p): Sl 1, k2tog, pass sl st over the k2tog.

Cast on a multiple of 10 sts plus 1.

Work preparation row (WS): *P5, mb, p4; rep from *, ending last rep p5.

Row 1 (RS): K1, *yo, k3, sl 1-k2tog-psso, k3, yo, k1; rep from * to end.

Row 2: Purl.

Row 3: P1, *k1, yo, k2, sl 1-k2tog-psso, k2, yo, k1, p1; rep from * to end.

Rows 4 and 6: *K1, p9; rep from * to last st, k1.

Row 5: P1, *k2, yo, k1, sl 1-k2tog-psso, k1, yo, k2, p1; rep from * to end.

Row 7: P1, *k3, yo, sl 1-k2tog-psso, yo, k3, p1; rep from * to end.

Row 8: Purl.

Row 9: K1, *k3, yo, sl 1-k2tog-psso, yo, k4; rep from * to end.

Continue from here with the pattern of your choice.

NOTE: For a more substantial edging, repeat rows 1–9 once more, and continue in your chosen pattern from there. Another option is to repeat rows 8 and 9 as your item's main pattern.

Floral Lace Edging

Here's a pretty edging that looks complex but is easy to work. This pattern begins with a wrong side row.

Sl 1-k2tog-psso (sk2p): Sl 1, k2tog, pass sl st over the k2tog.

Sl 1-k1-psso (skp): Sl 1, k1, pass sl st over the k1.

Cast on 13 sts.

Rows 1, 3, 5, and 7 (WS): K2, yo, k2tog, purl to end.

Row 2: Sl 1-k2tog-psso, yo, k2tog, yo, k1, yo, sl1-k1-psso, yo, k2, yo, k2tog, k1.

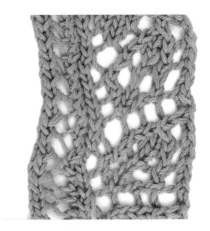

Row 4: [Sl 1-k1-psso, yo] twice, k1, [yo, k2tog] twice, k1, yo, k2tog, k1.

Row 6: Sl 1-k1-psso, yo, sl 1-k1-psso, k1, k2tog, yo, k1, yo, k2, yo, k2tog, k1.

Row 8: Sl 1-k1-psso, yo, sl 1-k2tog-psso, yo, k3, yo, k2, yo, k2tog, k1.

Rep rows 1–8 to desired length.

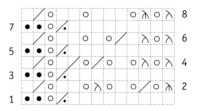

Diagonal Point Lace Trim

This is another pointed edging that is worked sideways: you work the pattern until it is the same length as the edge you'll attach it to. Try it on pillowcase hems, lampshades, girls' pajamas—the possibilities abound.

Cast on 15 sts.

Row 1: Sl 1, k1, yo, p2tog, k1, yo, k2tog, k3, yo, p2tog, k1, yo, k2.

Row 2: K2, p1, k1, yo, p2tog, k4, p1, k1, yo, p2tog, k2.

Row 3: Sl 1, k1, yo, p2tog, k2, yo, k2tog, k2, yo, p2tog, k2, yo, k2.

Row 4: K2, p1, k2, yo, p2tog, k3, p1, k2, yo, p2tog, k2.

Row 5: Sl 1, k1, yo, p2tog, k3, yo, k2tog, k1, yo, p2tog, k3, yo, k2.

Row 6: K2, p1, k3, yo, p2tog, k2, p1, k3, yo, p2tog, k2.

Row 7: Sl 1, k1, yo, p2tog, k4, yo, k2tog, yo, p2tog, k6.

Row 8: BO 3, k2, yo, p2tog, k1, p1, k4, yo, p2tog, k2.

Rep rows 1–8 for desired length.

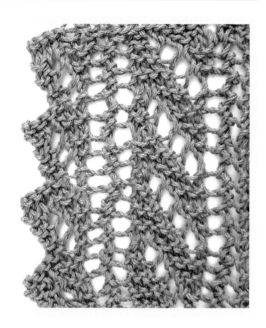

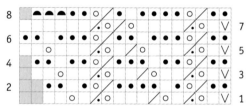

Ocean Waves

Work this lacy trim sideways until it is the same length as the edge you're attaching it to, and then just sew it on. It's the perfect edging for fancy linens, bedskirts, lacy curtains, and feminine sweaters. This one begins with a wrong side row.

Sl 1-k2tog-psso (sk2p): Sl 1, k2tog, pass sl st over the k2tog.

Cast on 13 sts.

Row 1 and all odd rows (WS): K2, purl to last 2 sts, k2.

Row 2 (RS): Sl 1, k3, yo, k5, yo, k2tog, yo, k2—15 sts.

Row 4: Sl 1, k4, sl 1-k2tog-psso, k2, [yo, k2tog] twice, k1—13 sts.

Row 6: Sl 1, k3, ssk, k2, [yo, k2tog] twice, k1—12 sts.

Row 8: Sl 1, k2, ssk, k2, [yo, k2tog] twice, k1.

Row 10: Sl 1, k1, ssk, k2 [yo, k2tog] twice, k1.

Row 12: K1, ssk, k2, yo, k1, yo, k2tog, yo, k2.

Row 14: Sl 1, [k3, yo] twice, k2tog, yo, k2.

Rep rows 1–14 to desired length.

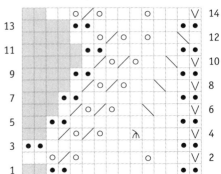

Diamond Eyelet Edging

Here the eyelets frame and highlight the diamond shapes on the edging. This is another edging that's worked sideways to the length desired. Note that the stitch count changes along the way, but returns to the original 9-stitch count by row 12.

Cast on 9 sts.

Row 1 (RS): K3, [k2tog, yo] twice, k1, yo, k1—10 sts.

Row 2 (WS): [K1, p1] 3 times, k4.

Row 3: K2, [k2tog, yo] twice, k3, yo, k1—11 sts.

Row 4: K1, p1, k3, p1, k1, p1, k3.

Row 5: K1, [k2tog, yo] twice, k5, yo, k1—12 sts.

Row 6: K1, p1, k5, p1, k1, p1, k2.

Row 7: K3, [yo, k2tog] twice, k1, k2tog, yo, k2tog—11 sts.

Row 8: K1, p1, k3, p1, k1, p1, k3.

Row 9: K4, yo, k2tog, yo, k3tog, yo, k2tog—10 sts.

Row 10: [K1, p1] 3 times, k4.

Row 11: K5, yo, k3tog, yo, k2tog—9 sts.

Row 12: [K1, p1] twice, k5.

Rep rows 1–12 to desired length.

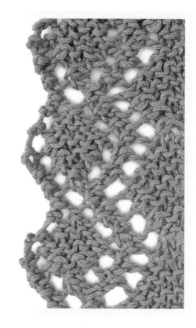

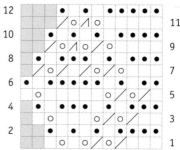

Loop Fringe Edging

Add a bit of fun to your hems, cuffs, and collars with this playful fringe. You can adjust the thickness of the fringe by tripling or quadrupling strands of yarn instead of doubling them. To create a shorter fringe, decrease the number of stitches at the end of row 1 and the beginning of row 2. This edging is worked sideways to the length desired, and sewn to your finished item.

Cast on 13 sts.

Row 1: K2, yo, k2tog, k1, yo, k2tog, k6.

Row 2: P5, k2, [yo, k2tog, k1] twice.

Rep rows 1 and 2 to desired length.

Next row: Sl 1, BO 7 sts, cut yarn and draw through st rem from BO. Sl rem 5 sts off needle and unravel down to CO row to form lps.

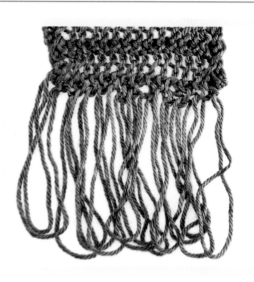

Palm Frond Edging

This beautiful edging, with its delicate single-strand "fronds," will dress up any item it adorns.

Cast on 10 sts and knit 1 row.

Row 1 (RS): Sl 1, k1, [yo, k2tog] twice, [yo] 4 times, k2tog, yo, p2tog.

Row 2: Yo, p2tog, k1, [k1, p1] twice (into the quadruple yarn over), [k1, p1] twice, k2.

Row 3: Sl 1, [k1, yo, k2tog] twice, k4, yo, p2tog.

Row 4: Yo, p2tog, k5, [p1, k2] twice.

Row 5: Sl 1, K1, yo, k2tog, k2, yo, k2tog, K3, yo, p2tog.

Row 6: Yo, p2tog, k4, p1, k3, p1, k2.

Row 7: Sl 1, k1, yo, k2tog, k3, yo, k2tog, k2, yo, p2tog.

Row 8: Yo, p2tog, k3, p1, k4, p1, k2.

Row 9: Sl 1, k1, yo, k2tog, k4, yo, k2tog, k1, yo, p2tog.

Row 10: Yo, p2tog, k2, p1, k5, p1, k2.

Row 11: Sl 1, k1, yo, k2tog, k5, yo, k2tog, yo, p2tog.

Row 12: BO 3; sl the st on the right needle to the left needle; yo, p2tog, k5, p1, k2.

Rep rows 1–12 to desired length.

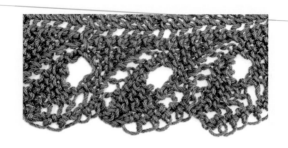

Netted Edging

This simple edging is a beautiful accompaniment to diaphanous scarves and wraps, or as a trim on half curtains and valances. It employs an unusual maneuver, 6 chain, which is described here. This edging begins with a wrong side row.

6 chain: Knit the next st, *then slip it back to the left needle and knit it again; rep from * 4 more times, having knit the same st 6 times.

Cast on 14 sts.

Row 1 (WS): K1, *yo, k2tog; rep from * to last st, yo, k1—15 sts.

Row 2 (RS): 6 chain, k1, pass the 6 chain st over the k1 and off the right needle, *yo, k2tog; rep from * to last st, k1.

Rep rows 1 and 2 to desired length.

Lacy Chevron Edging

Lend a three-dimensional effect to edges with this geometric trim. The stitch count nearly doubles by the time you're halfway through, and then returns to the original 7 stitches by the last row.

Cast on 7 sts.

Row 1: K2, [yo, k2tog] twice, yo, k1—8 sts.

Row 2 and all even rows to 20: Knit.

Row 3: K3, [yo, k2tog] twice, yo, k1—9 sts.

Row 5: K4, [yo, k2tog] twice, yo, k1—10 sts.

Row 7: K5, [yo, k2tog] twice, yo, k1—11 sts.

Row 9: K6, [yo, k2tog] twice, yo, k1—12 sts.

Row 11: K7, [yo, k2tog] twice, yo, k1—13 sts.

Row 13: K6, [yo, k2tog] twice, yo, k3tog—12 sts.

Row 15: K5, [yo, k2tog] twice, yo, k3tog—11 sts.

Row 17: K4, [yo, k2tog] twice, yo, k3tog—10 sts.

Row 19: K3 [yo, k2tog] twice, yo, k3tog—9 sts.

Row 21: K2, [yo, k2tog] twice, yo, k3tog—8 sts.

Row 22: K2tog, knit to end—7 sts.

Rep Rows 1–22 to desired length.

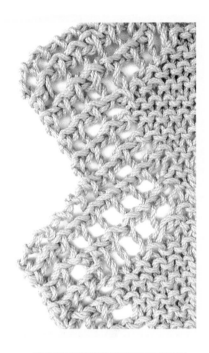

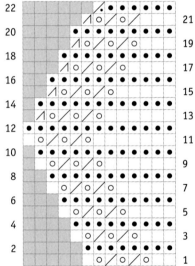

3-D Diamonds Edging

Here's an openwork edging that has a modern feel. Like many lace trims, this is worked sideways until it is the same length as the edge you'll be attaching it to.

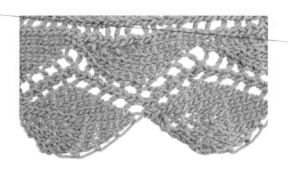

Sl 1-k2tog-psso (sk2p): Sl 1, k2tog, pass sl st over the k2tog.

Cast on 12 sts and purl 1 row.

Row 1: Sl 1, k1, yo, k2tog, p1, k4, yo, k2tog, yo, k1.

Rows 2, 4, 6, 8, and 10: Yo, purl to end.

Row 3: Sl 1, k1, yo, k2tog, p1, k2tog, k2, yo, k2tog, yo, k3.

Row 5: Sl 1, k1, yo, k2tog, p1, k2tog, k1, yo, k2tog, yo, k5.

Row 7: Sl 1, k1, yo, k2tog, p1, [k2tog, yo] twice, k7.

Row 9: Sl 1, k1, yo, k2tog [k2tog, yo] twice, k9.

Row 11: Sl 1, k1, yo, k2tog, k1, yo, k2tog, yo, k3, ssk, p1, k2tog, k3.

Rows 12, 14, 16and 18: Purl.

Row 13: Sl 1, k1, yo, k2tog, k2, yo, k2tog, yo, k2, ssk, p1, k2tog, k2.

Row 15: Sl 1, k1, yo, k2tog, k3, yo, k2tog, yo, k1, ssk, p1, k2tog, k1.

Row 17: Sl 1, k1, yo, k2tog, k4, yo, k2tog, yo, ssk, p1, k2tog.

Row 19: Sl 1, k1, yo, k2tog, k5, yo, k2tog, yo, sl 1-k2tog-psso.

Row 20: P2tog, purl to end.

Rep rows 1–20 for desired length.

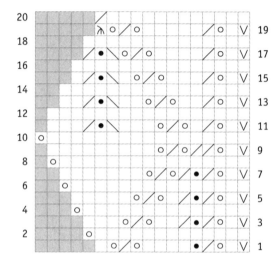

Picot Hem

A picot hem, which looks like a line of tiny scallops and is easy to do, adds that extra polish to anything you choose to use it for—bags, baby knits and blankets, or tailored skirts and jackets. You need two sets of needles: one suited to your yarn's gauge, and the other a size or two smaller.

Using the smaller needles, cast on an odd number of sts.

Inside hem: Work in stockinette stitch (knit on RS, purl on WS) for approximately 1 inch, ending with a WS row.

Change to the larger needles.

Picot row: *K2tog, yo; rep from * to last st, k1.

Outside hem: Beg with a WS row, continue in stockinette st for 1 inch.

When your knit item is complete, lightly steam folded hem, and whipstitch the inside edge in place.

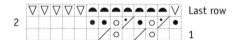

CHAPTER 9

Creative Stitches and Combinations

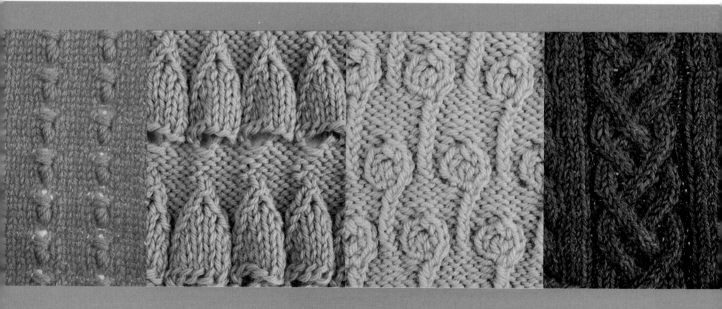

Loop Stitch

You can use this technique to add fun and fashionable borders to sweater hems, collars, and cuffs; it also works fabulously for cushion covers. It may take a little practice to master, so the loop instructions are given in great detail. This pattern begins with a wrong side row.

Loop 1: Knit into next st, but don't drop it off the needle. Bring yarn to front, between the needles, and loop it over your thumb, then bring the yarn between the needles to the back. Knit into the st again, this time bringing it up and off the left needle. You will have 2 sts on the right needle. Pass the 1st st over the 2nd and off to secure the loop.

Cast on any number of sts.

Row 1 (WS): Knit.

Row 2 (RS): *Loop 1; rep from * to end.

Rep rows 1 and 2 for loop stitch.

Acorns

Here's a fun pattern that requires a bit of patience and concentration, but is well worth the effort. Once you master making the little "acorns," you can disperse them across the fabric in the pattern as you wish.

Cast on a multiple of 5 sts plus 2.

Rows 1 and 3 (RS): Knit.

Row 2 and all even rows (WS): Purl.

Row 5: K2, *make acorn [insert right needle into the st 4 rows below the 3rd st on left needle, draw up a lp, place lp onto left needle, yo on right needle] 3 times, but omit the yo in the 3rd rep, knit the 3 long sts plus the next st on left needle tog tbl, pass both yarn overs on right needle over the last st worked (making the acorn "cap"), k4; rep from * to end.

Row 6: Purl.

Rep rows 1–6 for acorns.

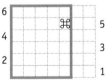

Bluebell Stitch

Purling 5 stitches together and then increasing 5 stitches into the following stitch forms the bell-shaped motifs in this eye-catching pattern.

Cast on a multiple of 6 sts plus 2.

Row 1 (WS): K1, *p5tog, (k1, p1, k1, p1, k1) into next st; rep from * to last st, k1.

Rows 2 and 4 (RS): Purl.

Row 3: K1, *(k1, p1, k1, p1, k1) into next st, p5tog; rep from * to last st, k1.

Row 5: *Insert right needle into 1st st, wrap yarn around needle 3 times and knit the st; rep from * to end.

Row 6: *Knit the first of the 3 wraps and drop the other 2; rep from * for every st. (You should have the same number of sts that you began with.)

Rep rows 1–6 for bluebell stitch.

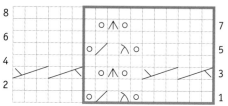

Cabled Lace

You can combine various types of stitches to form intricate and unique patterns. Here's a fairly simple blend of basic cables and eyelets.

C6B: Sl next 3 sts to cn and hold at front of work, k3 from left needle, k3 from cn.

Sl 1-k1-psso (skp): Sl 1, k1, pass sl st over the k1.

Sl 2-k1-p2sso (s2kp): Sl the 1st and 2nd sts tog kwise, k1, pass the 2 sl sts over the knit st.

Cast on a multiple of 11 sts plus 6.

Rows 1 and 5 (RS): K6, *yo, sl 1-k1-psso, k1, k2tog, yo, k6; rep from * to end.

Row 2 and all even rows (WS): Purl.

Row 3: *C6B, k1, yo, sl 2-k1-p2sso, yo, k1; rep from * to last 6 sts, C6B.

Row 7: *K7, yo, sl 2-k1-p2sso, yo, k1; rep from * to last 6 sts, k6.

Row 8: Purl.

Rep rows 1–8 for cabled lace.

Smocking Stitch

Smocking stitch works beautifully on sweater bodices, little girls' dresses, and cushion covers.

Smock st: Insert right needle between 6th and 7th sts on left needle, wrap yarn over needle as if to knit and draw lp through; place lp on left needle and knit it together with next st.

Cast on a multiple of 16 sts plus 2.

Rows 1 and 5 (RS): P2, *k2, p2; rep from * to end.

Rows 2, 4, and 6 (WS): *K2, p2; rep from * to last 2 sts, k2.

Row 3: P2, *smock st, k1, p2, k2, p2; rep from * to end.

Row 7: P2, k2, p2, *smock st, k1, p2, k2, p2; rep from * to last 4 sts, k2, p2.

Row 8: Rep row 2.

Rep rows 1–8 for smocking stitch.

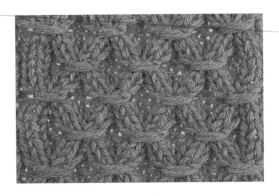

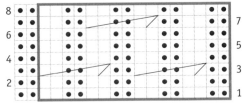

Lace Curtains

This pattern is similar to feather and fan, also known as *peacock stitch,* in that you pair increases and decreases continuously across the rows to create this dynamic fabric that is just the thing for café curtains, lined skirts, and elegant wraps.

Cast on a multiple of 12 sts plus 1.

Rows 1–4: Knit.

Rows 5, 7, 9, and 11: K1, *[k2tog] twice, [yo, k1] 3 times, yo, [ssk] twice, k1; rep from * to end.

Rows 6, 8, 10, and 12: Purl.

Repeat rows 1–12 for lace curtains.

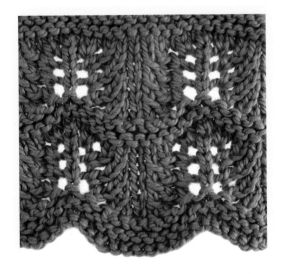

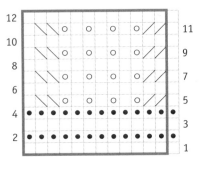

Clusters of Wheat

This stitch pattern is like a basketweave with the simple addition of wrapping 4 stitches. You can see how the addition of a minor detail can markedly alter a plain pattern.

Wrap 4: Insert right needle between 4th and 5th sts on left needle and draw up a long lp, k4, pass long lp over the 4 knit sts to wrap.

Cast on a multiple of 6 sts plus 1.

Row 1 (RS): *K4, p2; rep from * to last st, k1.

Rows 2 and 4 (WS): P1, *k2, p4; rep from * to end.

Row 3: *Wrap 4, p2; rep from * to last st, k1.

Rows 5 and 11: Knit.

Row 6: Purl.

Row 7: K1, *p2, k4; rep from * to end.

Rows 8 and 10: *P4, k2; rep from * to last st, p1.

Row 9: K1, *p2, wrap 4; rep from * to end.

Row 12: Purl.

Rep rows 1–12 for clusters of wheat.

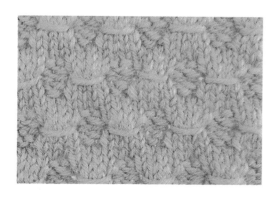

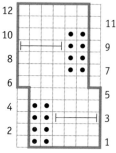

Gothic Arches

Here's a pretty pattern that forms from mere decreases and eyelets.

Sl 1-k1-psso (skp): Sl 1, k1, pass sl st over the k1.

Cast on a multiple of 11 sts plus 3.

Row 1 (RS): K4, *k2tog, yo, p2, yo, sl 1-k1-psso, k5; rep from *, ending last rep k4.

Row 2 and all even rows (WS): Work sts as they appear, purling the yarn overs.

Row 3: K3, *k2tog, yo, k1, p2, k1, yo, sl 1-k1-psso, k3; rep from * to end.

Row 5: K2, *k2tog, yo, k2, p2, k2, yo, sl 1-k1-psso, k1; rep from *, ending last rep k2.

Row 7: K1, k2tog, *yo, k3, p2, k3, yo, k3tog; rep from *, ending last rep sl 1-k1-psso, k1 (instead of k3tog).

Rows 9 and 11: K2, *yo, k2, k2tog, p2, sl 1-k1-psso, k2, yo, k1; rep from *, ending last rep k2.

Row 12: Rep row 2.

Rep rows 1–12 for gothic arches.

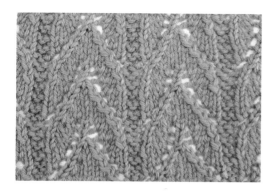

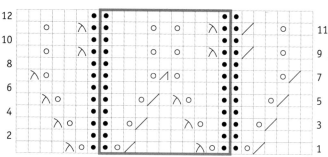

Mirrored Leaves

A lovely scalloped hem forms as you work this pattern.

Sl 1-k1-psso (skp): Sl 1, k1, pass sl st over the k1.

Cast on a multiple of 24 sts plus 1.

Row 1 (RS): K1, *m1, sl 1-k1-psso, k4, k2tog, k3, m1, k1, m1, k3, sl 1-k1-psso, k4, k2tog, m1, k1; rep from * to end.

Row 2 and all even rows (WS): Purl.

Row 3: K1, *m1, k1, sl 1-k1-psso, k2, k2tog, k4, m1, k1, m1, k4, sl 1-k1-psso, k2, k2tog, k1, m1, k1; rep from * to end.

Row 5: K1, *m1, k2, sl 1-k1-psso, k2tog, k5, m1, k1, m1, k5, sl 1-k1-psso, k2tog, k2, m1, k1; rep from * to end.

Row 7: K1, *m1, k3, sl 1-k1-psso, k4, k2tog, m1, k1, m1, sl 1-k1-psso, k4, k2tog, k3, m1, k1; rep from * to end.

Row 9: K1, *m1, k4, sl 1-k1-psso, k2, k2tog, [k1, m1] twice, k1, sl 1-k1-psso, k2, k2tog, k4, m1, k1; rep from * to end.

Row 11: K1, *m1, k5, sl 1-k1-psso, k2tog, k2, m1, k1, m1, k2, sl 1-k1-psso, k2tog, k5, m1, k1; rep from * to end.

Row 12: Rep row 2.

Rep rows 1–12 for mirrored leaves.

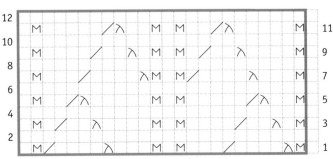

Bells in Rows

Here's a pattern made up of highly embossed bell motifs. You can use one row of bells as a decorative border for sweater hems, cuffs, and collars, or repeat the bell rows as an allover pattern.

Cast on a multiple of 4 sts.

Row 1 (RS): Purl.

Row 2 (WS): Knit.

Row 3: P4, *CO 8 sts using backward loop method, p4; rep from * to end.

Row 4: K4, *purl the 8 CO sts, k4; rep from * to end.

Row 5: P4, *k8, p4; rep from * to end.

Row 6: K4, *p8, k4; rep from * to end.

Row 7: P4, *ssk, k4, k2tog, p4; rep from * to end.

Row 8: K4, *p6, k4; rep from * to end.

Row 9: P4, *ssk, k2, k2tog, p4; rep from * to end.

Row 10: K4, *p4, k4; rep from * to end.

Row 11: P4, *ssk, k2tog, p4; rep from * to end.

Row 12: K4, *p2, k4; rep from * to end.

Row 13: P4, *k2tog, p4; rep from * to end.

Row 14: K4, *p1, k4; rep from * to end.

Row 15: P4, *k2tog, p3; rep from * to end.

Row 16: Knit.

Rep rows 1–16 for bells in rows.

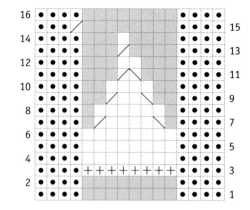

Lollipops

This pattern employs twisted stitches and 4-stitch increases and decreases to form the lollipops.

Sl 2-k3tog-p2sso (s2k3p): Slip the 1st and 2nd sts tog kwise, k3tog, pass the 2 sl sts over the k3tog.

Cast on a multiple of 6 sts plus 1.

Rows 1 and 3 (RS): *P5, k1 tbl; rep from * to last 2 sts, p2.

Rows 2 and 4 (WS): K2, *p1 tbl, k5; rep from * to end.

Row 5: *P5, [k1, p1, k1, p1, k1] into next st; rep from * to last 2 sts, p2.

Row 6: K2, *p5, k5; rep from * to end.

Row 7: *P2, k1 tbl, p2, k5; rep from * to last 2 sts, p2.

Row 8: K2, *p5, k2, p1 tbl, k2; rep from * to end.

Row 9: *P2, k1 tbl, p2, sl 2-k3tog-p2sso; rep from * to end.

Rows 10 and 12: *K5, p1 tbl; rep from * to last 2 sts, k2.

Row 11: P2, *k1 tbl, p5; rep from * to end.

Row 13: P2, *[k1, p1, k1, p1, k1] into next st, p5; rep from * to end.

Row 14: *K5, p5; rep from * to last 2 sts, k2.

Row 15: P2, *k5, p2, k1 tbl, p2; rep from * to end.

Row 16: K2, *p1 tbl, k2, p5, k2; rep from * to end.

Row 17: P2, *sl 2-k3tog-p2sso, p2, k1 tbl, p2; rep from * to end.

Row 18: Rep row 4.

Rep rows 3–18 for lollipops.

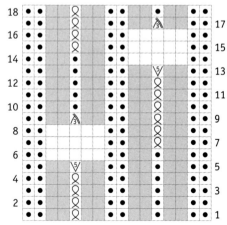

Feather and Fan Cable Panel

You can use this highly textured pattern as 36-stitch panel for pullovers, scarves, and afghans or use it as an allover pattern by casting on a multiple of 34 stitches plus 2.

C4F: Sl next 2 sts to cn and hold at front of work, k2 from left needle, k2 from cn.

C4B: Sl next 2 sts to cn and hold at back of work, k2 from left needle, k2 from cn.

Cast on a multiple of 34 sts plus 2.

Row 1 (RS): *P2, k4, [p2tog] twice, [yo, k1] 4 times, [p2tog] 4 times, [k1, yo] 4 times, [p2tog] twice, k4; rep from * to last 2 sts, p2.

Row 2 (WS): K2, *p32, k2; rep from * to end.

Row 3: *P2, C4F, k24, C4B; rep from * to last 2 sts, p2.

Row 4: Rep row 2.

Rep rows 1–4 for feather and fan cable panel.

Rope and Braid Cable Panel (37-Stitch Panel)

Here's a panel that incorporates three different cables. It begins with a wrong side row.

C4B: Sl next 2 sts to cn and hold at back of work, k2 from left needle, k2 from cn.

C4F: Sl next 2 sts to cn and hold at front of work, k2 from left needle, k2 from cn.

C5B: Sl next 3 sts to cn and hold at back, k2 from left needle, sl the purl st from the cn back onto left needle and purl it, k2 rem sts from cn.

C5F: Sl next 3 sts to cn and hold at front, k2 from left needle, sl the purl st from the cn back onto left needle and purl it, k2 rem sts from cn.

C6B: Sl next 3 sts to cn and hold at back of work, k3 from left needle, k3 from cn.

C6F: Sl next 3 sts to cn and hold at front of work, k3 from left needle, k3 from cn.

3-st LPC: Sl next 2 sts to cn and hold at front, p1 from left needle, k2 from cn.

3-st RPC: Sl next st to cn and hold at back, k2 from left needle, p1 from cn.

Rows 1, 3, 9, and 11 (WS): P6, k1, p3, [k2, p2] twice, k1, [p2, k2] twice, p3, k1, p6.

Row 2 (RS): C6B, p1, k3, p2, k2, p2, C5B, p2, k2, p2, k3, p1, C6F.

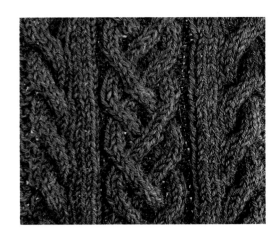

Rows 4 and 12: K6, p1, k3, p2, 3-st LPC, 3-st RPC, p1, 3-st LPC, 3-st RPC, p2, k3, p1, k6.

Rows 5, 7, 13, and 15: P6, k1, p3, [k3, p4] twice, k3, p3, k1, p6.

Rows 6 and 14: K6, p1, k3, p3, C4B, p3, C4F, p3, k3, p1, k6.

Row 8: K6, p1, k3, p2, 3-st RPC, 3-st LPC, p1, 3-st RPC, 3-st LPC, p2, k3, p1, k6.

Row 10: C6B, p1, k3, p2, k2, p2, C5F, p2, k2, p2, k3, p1, C6F.

Row 16: Rep row 8.

Rep rows 1–16 for rope and braid cable panel.

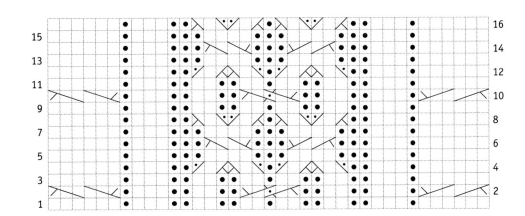

Eyelet Diamond Cable and Bobble Panel (33-Stitch Panel)

This versatile combination of openwork, bobbles, and cables works as an insert for a sweater pattern. You can also use it as a repeat for a pretty bedspread.

Sl 1-k1-psso (skp): Sl 1, k1, pass sl st over the k1.

Sl 1-k2tog-psso (sk2p): Sl 1, k2tog, pass sl st over the k2tog.

M7 (begin bobble): Knit into front, back, front, back, front, back, and front of next st.

Dec 7-to-1 (complete bobble): Sl next 6 bobble sts to right needle, k1 (7th bobble st), pass the 6 slipped bobble sts on right needle one at a time over the 7th st and off.

C4F: Sl next 2 sts to cn and hold at front of work, k2 from left needle, k2 from cn.

Row 1 (RS): P1, k4, p1, k9, yo, sl 1-k2tog-psso, yo, k9, p1, k4, p1.

Rows 2, 6, 10, and 14 (WS): K1, p4, k1, p1, m7, p17, m7, p1, k1, p4, k1.

Row 3: P1, C4F, p1, k1, dec 7-to-1, k5, k2tog, yo, k3, yo, sl 1-k1-psso, k5, dec 7-to-1, k1, p1, C4F, p1.

Row 4: K1, p4, k1, p3, m7, p13, m7, p3, k1, p4, k1.

Row 5: P1, k4, p1, k3, dec 7-to-1, k2, k2tog, yo, k5, yo, sl 1-k1-psso, k2, dec 7-to-1, k3, p1, k4, p1.

Row 7: P1, C4F, p1, k1, dec 7-to-1, k3, k2tog, yo, k7, yo, sl 1-k1-psso, k3, dec 7-to-1, k1, p1, C4F, p1.

Row 8: K1, p4, k1, p21, k1, p4, k1.

Row 9: P1, k4, p1, k6, yo, sl 1-k1-psso, k5, k2tog, yo, k6, p1, k4, p1.

Row 11: P1, C4F, p1, k1, dec 7-to-1, k5, yo, sl 1-k1-psso, k3, k2tog, yo, k5, dec 7-to-1, k1, p1, C4F, p1.

Row 12: K1, p4, k1, p3, m7, p13, m7, p3, k1, p4, k1.

Row 13: P1, k4, p1, k3, dec 7-to-1, k4, yo, sl 1-k1-psso, k1, k2tog, yo, k4, dec 7-to-1, k3, p1, k4, p1.

Row 15: P1, C4F, p1, k1, dec 7-to-1, k7, yo, sl 1-k2tog-psso, yo, k7, dec 7-to-1, k1, p1, C4F, p1.

Row 16: K1, p4, k1, p21, k1, p4, k1.

Rep rows 1–16 for eyelet diamond cable and bobble panel.

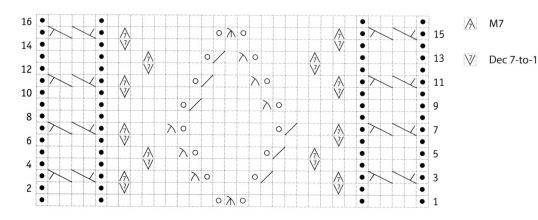

	A	M7
	V	Dec 7-to-1

Twig Panel (39-Stitch Panel)

This wide panel, which employs twisted stitches, cables, eyelets, and a knot, is the perfect centerpiece for a bulky pullover or dress.

RTp: K2tog and leave on needle, insert needle between 1st and 2nd sts and purl 1st st, then drop both original sts from left needle.

LTp: Skip 1st st, purl 2nd st tbl from back of work and leave on needle, bring yarn to front and knit 1st st tbl, then drop both original sts from left needle.

C4B: Sl next 2 sts to cn and hold at back of work, k2 from left needle, k2 from cn.

C4F: Sl next 2 sts to cn and hold at front of work, k2 from left needle, k2 from cn.

Sl 1-k2tog-psso (sk2p): Sl 1, k2tog, pass sl st over the k2tog.

Row 1 (RS): P2, ssk, yo, p1, k4, p1, yo, k2tog, p5, RTp, k1, LTp, p5, ssk, yo, p1, k4, p1, yo, k2tog, p2.

Row 2 and all even rows (WS): Work sts as they appear.

Row 3: P2, ssk, yo, p1, C4B, p1, yo, k2tog, p4, RTp, p1, k1, p1, LTp, p4, ssk, yo, p1, C4F, p1, yo, k2tog, p2.

Row 5: P2, ssk, yo, p1, k4, p1, yo, k2tog, p3, RTp, p2, k1, p2, LTp, p3, ssk, yo, p1, k4, p1, yo, k2tog, p2.

Row 7: P2, ssk, yo, p1, k4, p1, yo, k2tog, p2, RTp, p3, k1, p3, LTp, p2, ssk, yo, p1, k4, p1, yo, k2tog, p2.

Row 9: P2, ssk, yo, p1, C4B, p1, yo, k2tog, p2, kfbf, p4, k1, p4, kfbf, p2, ssk, yo, p1, C4F, p1, yo, k2tog, p2.

Row 11: P2, ssk, yo, p1, k4, p1, yo, k2tog, p2, sl 1-k2tog-psso, p4, k1, p4, sl 1-k2tog-psso, p2, ssk, yo, p1, k4, p1, yo, k2tog, p2.

Rep rows 1–12 for twig panel.

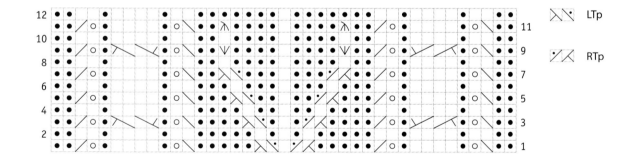

CHAPTER 10

Color
Knitting

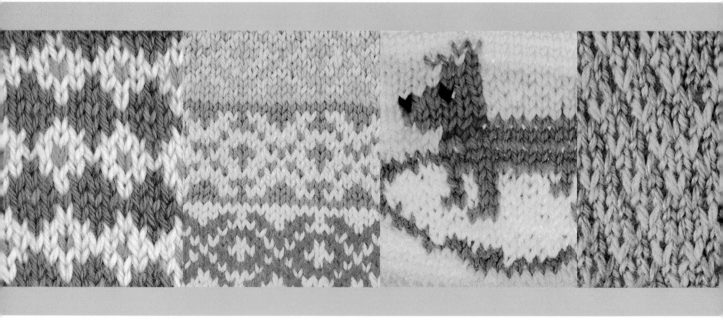

Stranded Color Pattern 1

This eye-catching design will really liven up a pair of socks or a simple sleeveless pullover.

8 stitches, 8-row repeat

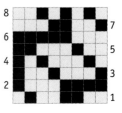

Stranded Color Pattern 2

Simply varying the heights of the rectangles lends this pattern its modern appeal.

3 stitches, 7-row repeat

Stranded Color Pattern 3

Use this as an allover pattern to complement a detailed border.
Finish with row 1 for the final repetition.

7 stitches, 7-row repeat

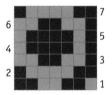

Stranded Color Pattern 4

After working a few repetitions of this striking pattern,
you'll be able to do it without having to think about it.

12 stitches, 16-row repeat

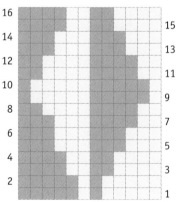

Stranded Color Pattern 5

This color pattern is unusual in that you use two colors *and* you knit and purl all in the same row. To work the purl stitches on the right side after knitting the first two stitches, drop the first color and leave it at the back, then bring the second color under the first and to the front of the work. Purl the two stitches, then return the second color to the back. On the wrong side, bring the second yarn to the back, knit the first two stitches, then bring the same yarn to the front. Now purl two stitches with the first color.

4 stitches, 2-row repeat

Stranded Color Pattern 6

This pattern can be used as a border when worked over the full six rows, or it can be used as an allover stripe pattern if you repeat rows 1 through 5.

6 stitches, 6-row border or 5-row repeat

Stranded Color Pattern 7

This is a very easy allover pattern that, up close, looks like tiny *fleurs-de-lis*.

6 stitches, 4-row repeat

Stranded Color Pattern 8

You can use this pattern as a border accent at the hem or cuff of a sweater.

8 stitches, 11-row border

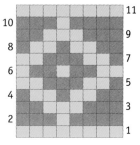

Stranded Color Pattern 9

Liven up a plain stockinette stitch sweater with this simple border. To use it as an allover pattern, repeat rows 1 through 6 and finish the final repetition with row 7.

4 stitches, 7-row border or 6-row repeat

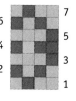

Stranded Color Pattern 10

This allover pattern is so simple to work, but the result is distinctively modern.

4 stitches, 12-row repeat

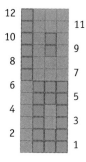

Stranded Color Pattern 11

This leaf-patterned border is perfect for dressing up cuffs of mittens and gloves.

4 stitches, 15-row border

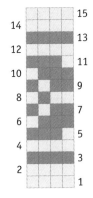

Stranded Color Pattern 12

This simple allover pattern is good for sweaters, vests, mittens—just about everything, really. You can change the colors to suit the project.

4 stitches, 6-row repeat

Stranded Color Pattern 13

This pattern is easy to work but looks richer because you use four colors. Use it as a border, as an allover pattern, or as a stripe in a Fair Isle sweater.

6 stitches, 7-row repeat

Stranded Color Pattern 14

As a 15-row border, this pattern is fairly staid; as an allover pattern, it's electrifying. To work it as a border, end with row 1.

4 stitches, 14-row repeat or 15-row border

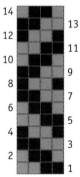

Stranded Color Pattern 15

A simple check pattern like this works wonderfully for blankets, pillow covers, and plain pullovers.

6 stitches, 12-row repeat

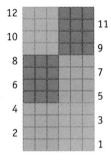

Stranded Color Pattern 16

Here you can see how changing the color combinations of the same stitch pattern can drastically change the look of the design. Repeating the same pattern as stripes in different colors is also a fun way to make a very colorful pattern without a lot of fuss.

8 stitches, 33-row repeat

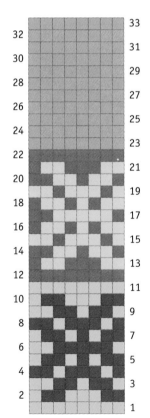

Stranded Color Pattern 17

This pattern is presented as a vertical panel so that you can use it for a vertical border along cardigan fronts, up the side of socks, as a central panel on a multicolor sweater, or as a gusset for a handbag.

19 stitches, 16-row repeat

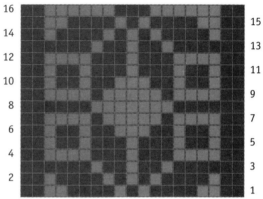

Stranded Color Pattern 18

This is a pretty flower-motif border pattern that can be
turned clockwise on its side to be used as a vertical panel.

20 stitches, 19-row border

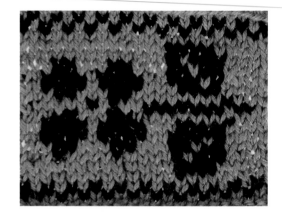

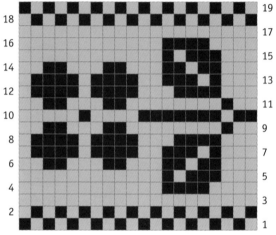

Stranded Color Pattern 19

This is the color version of the Circles pattern on page 32.

8 stitches plus 1, 8-row repeat

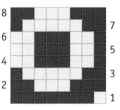

Stranded Color Pattern 20

There are many versions of argyle. This one is monochromatic, but you can change the color scheme to suit your taste.

12 stitches, 10-row repeat

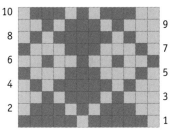

Stranded Color Pattern 21

In any combination of colors, this pattern creates a vibrant fabric that's ideal for cushion covers, mittens, and children's wear.

10 stitches, 10-row repeat

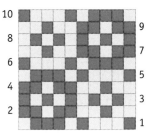

Stranded Color Pattern 22

This is the perfect border for ski sweaters and matching mittens.

12 stitches, 19-row border

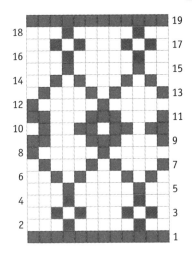

Stranded Color Pattern 23

Use this bold border for fall coats and hems of sweaters, skirts, and dresses.

12 stitches, 21-row border

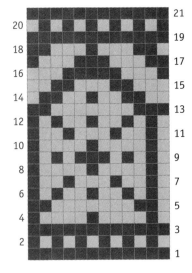

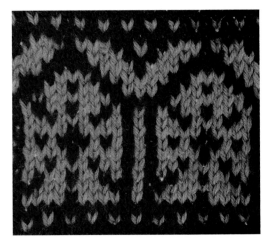

Stranded Color Pattern 24

This pattern, with its border of ocean waves and anchor motif, works perfectly in denim or cotton yarn for a summer pullover. To use it as a border, eliminate row 31.

16 stitches, 31-row repeat

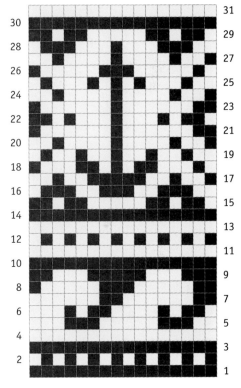

Stranded Color Pattern 25

To use this as a border, work the 28 rows, then repeat rows 1 through 6 to complete it.

30 stitches, 28-row repeat

Stranded Color Pattern 26

Here are two patterns in one. You can repeat the entire
27 rows over and over for a striped design, or, after finishing the first 27 rows, repeat rows 11 through 27 as the
allover pattern.

14 stitches, 27-row repeat

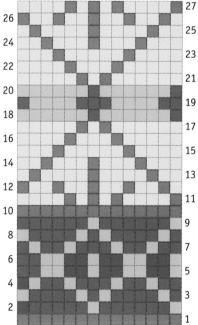

Stranded Color Pattern 27

Here's another two-for-one design. You can work the full 33 rows over and over as the pattern or, after working the first 33 rows, repeat rows 15 through 33 as the allover design.

28 stitches plus 1, 33-row repeat

Stranded Color Pattern 28

This design works well as a decorative pillow cover. Or use it as an allover pattern for a Scandinavian-style sweater.

22 stitches, 27-row repeat

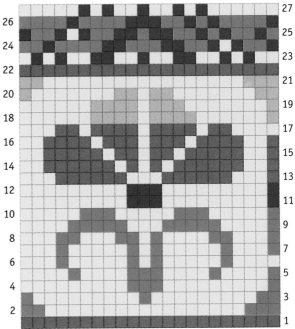

Stranded Color Pattern 29

Use this pattern for a striking men's pullover. Also,
geometric designs like this one always work well for
bags—from roomy totes to tiny change purses.

20 stitches, 24-row repeat

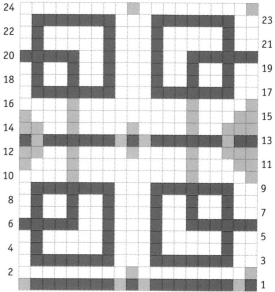

Stranded Color Pattern 30

Knit some sample swatches of this lively pattern in a few different color schemes and you'll see how versatile it is.

20 stitches, 20-row repeat

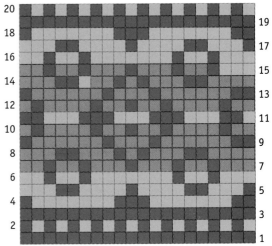

Stranded Color Pattern 31

Here's another pattern that you can work as it is, or take it apart and use the first 18 rows alone as a border.

32 stitches, 37-row repeat

Stranded Color Pattern 32

A warm winter sweater knit up in this design will remind you that spring will eventually come.

14 stitches, 21-row repeat

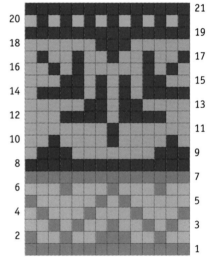

Stranded Color Pattern 33

Though this pattern is good for just about anything, it is very well suited to things you knit for the home—like placemats, cushion covers, bath mats, and chair pads.

26 stitches, 24-row repeat

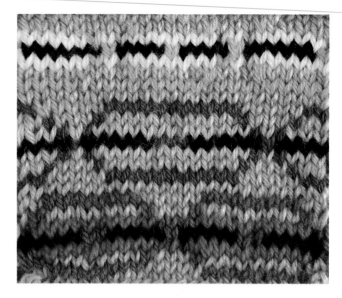

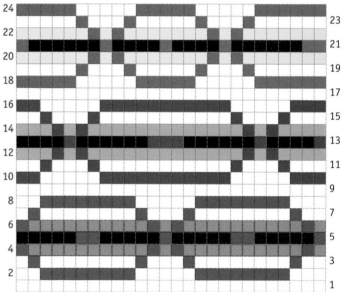

Stranded Color Pattern 34

This is the perfect pattern for a densely knit ski sweater.

20 stitches, 36-row repeat

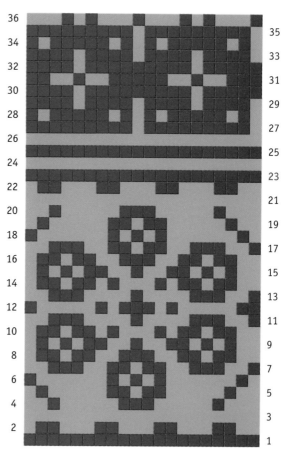

Stranded Color Pattern 35

This is a big pattern worthy of oversized thigh-length pullovers, long skirts, and hefty floor cushions.

34 stitches, 40-row repeat

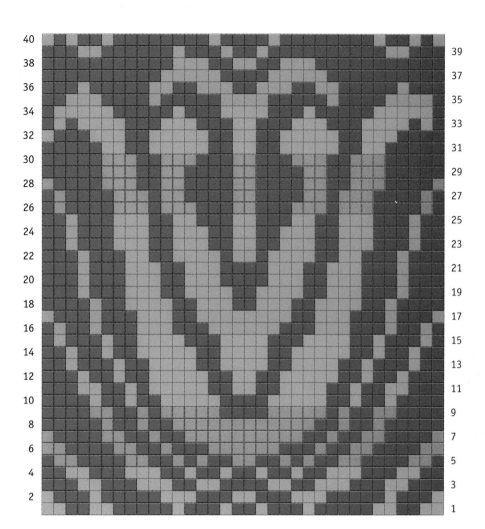

Stranded Color Pattern 36

This allover pattern involves using more than two colors per row. You can carry all four yarns across the back as you would with two.

36 stitches, 36-row repeat

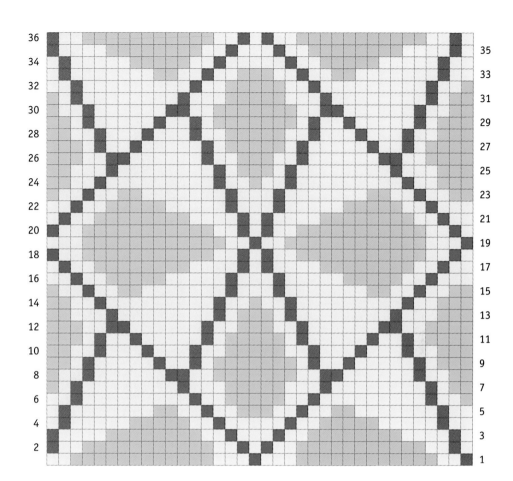

Stranded Color Pattern 37

An allover pattern like this takes a bit of concentration to work at first, but after a few repeats the diagonals become predictable and the beauty of the pattern unfolding keeps you going.

36 stitches, 36-row repeat

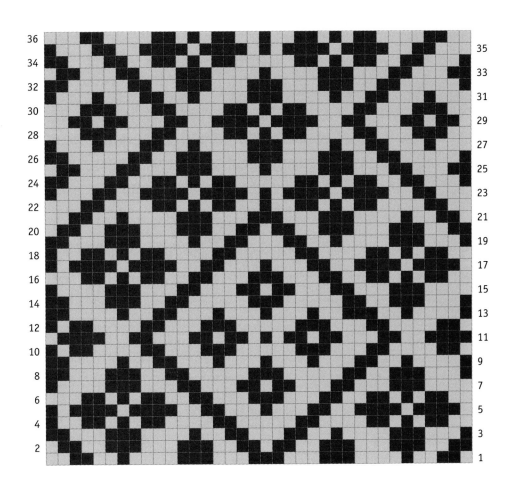

Heart

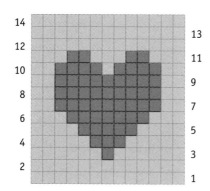

Star

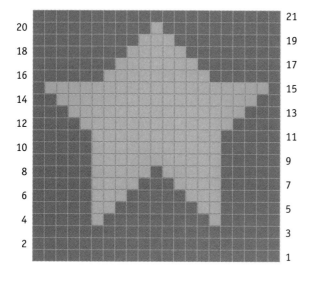

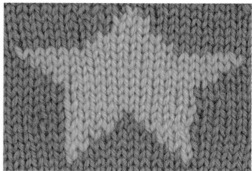

Duck

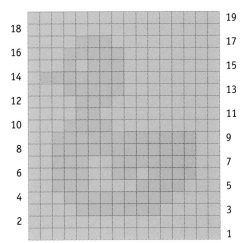
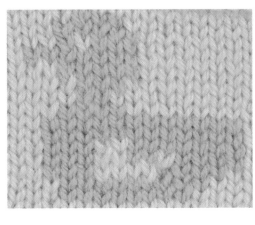

Butterfly

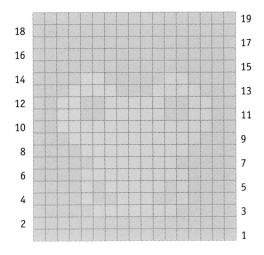
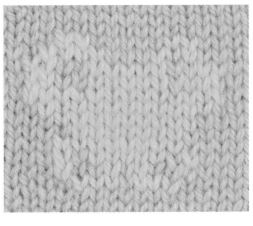

Flower

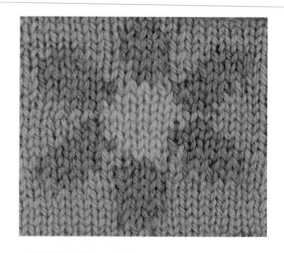

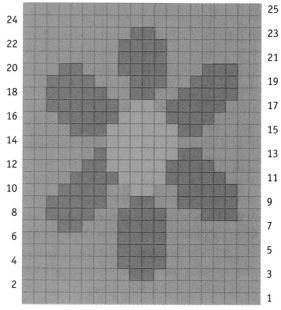

Bird

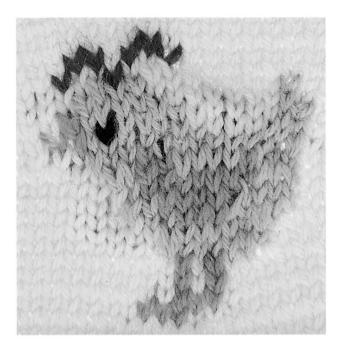

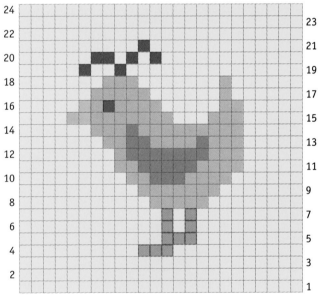

Sailboat

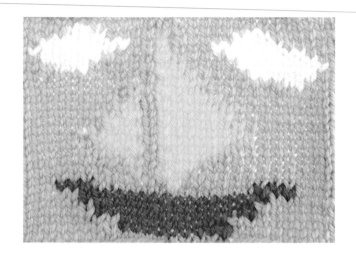

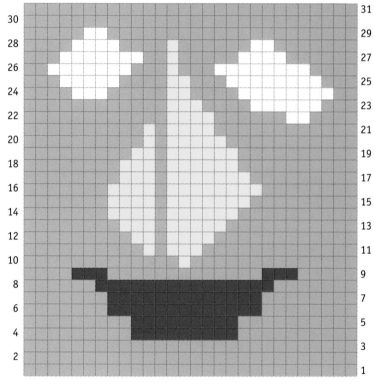

Blue Cat

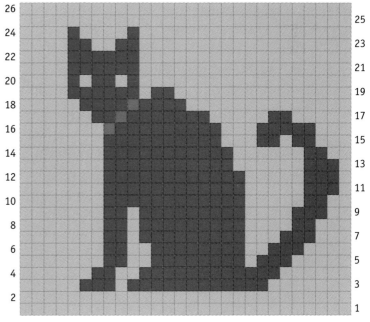

Dog

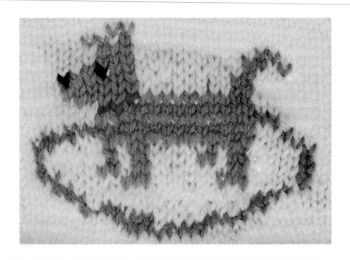

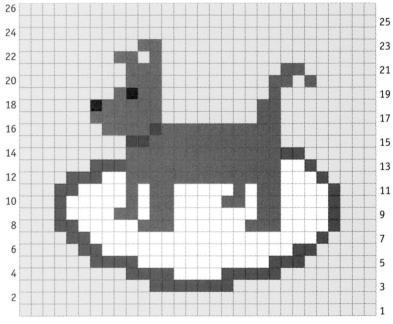

Snowflake

Rose

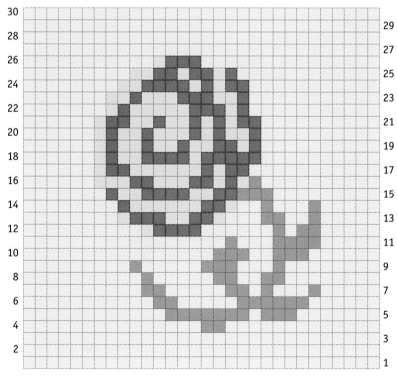

Friends

Teapot with Flower

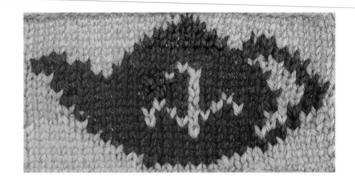

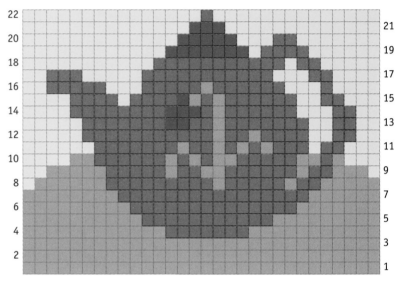

Robot

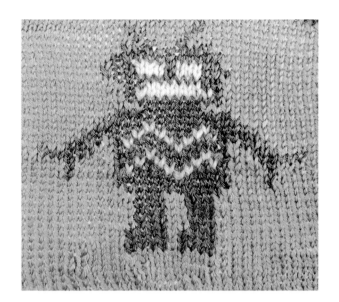

Planet

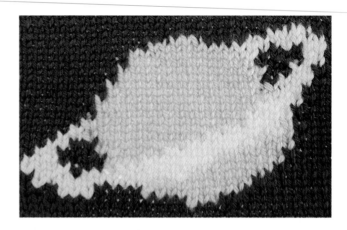

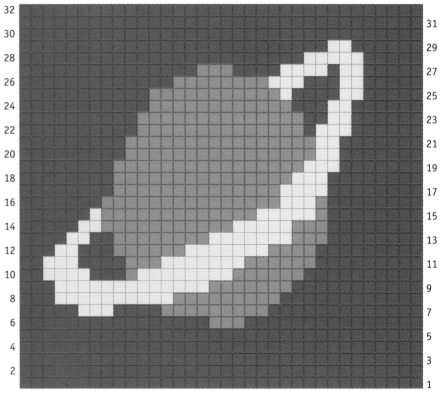

Flower Pot

Petrushka

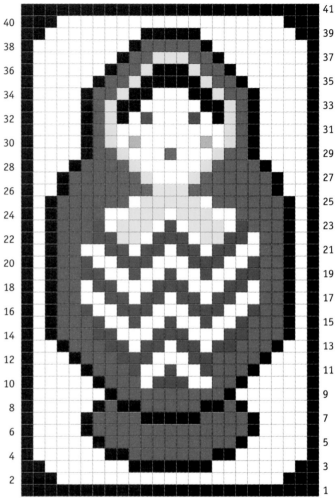

Color-Slip Pattern 1

24 stitches, 12-row repeat

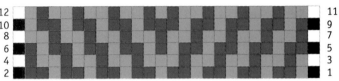

Color-Slip Pattern 2

10 stitches plus 1, 28-row repeat

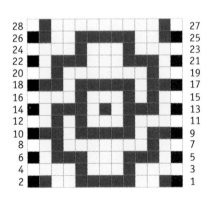

Color-Slip Pattern 3

16 stitches, 32-row repeat

Color-Slip Pattern 4

12 stitches, 24-row repeat

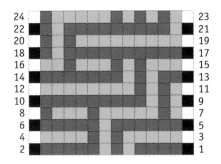

Color-Slip Pattern 5

16 stitches, 32-row repeat

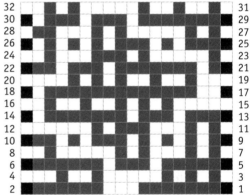

Color-Slip Pattern 6

11 stitches, 36-row repeat

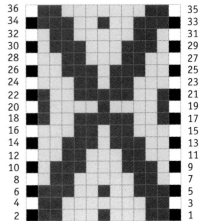

Color-Slip Pattern 7

14 stitches, 24-row repeat

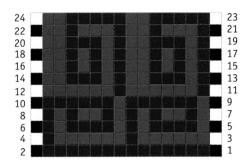

Color-Slip Pattern 8

12 stitches plus 1, 24-row repeat

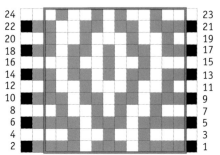

Color-Slip Pattern 9

12 stitches plus 1, 32-row repeat

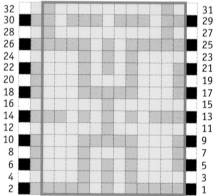